the Journey of Marriage

✤ IN THE ORTHODOX CHURCH ✤

Philip Mamalakis
and
Charles Joanides

foreword
by
His Eminence Archbishop DEMETRIOS
Primate of the Greek Orthodox Church in America

design and illustration
by
kanakarisdesign

Greek Orthodox Archdiocese of America

The Journey of Marriage in the Orthodox Church
by Philip Mamalakis and Charles Joanides

©2010, 2012, 2015 by Greek Orthodox Archdiocese of America
New York, 10075
www.goarch.org
First edition 2010; Second edition 2012; Third edition 2015

Illustrations by Kanakaris design.
All rights reserved.

79 Saint Basil Road Garrison NY 10524
Phone. 845.424.0175/Fax. 845.424.1175
familycare@goarch.org

ISBN 978-1-58438-026-9

The copyright holders retain all rights to this work. No part of this publication may be reproduced, stored in retrieval system, or transmitted in any form or by any means—electronic, mechanical, photocopy, recording, or any other—without the prior written permission of the publisher. Limited excerpts may be reproduced without permission if the appropriate credit is given.

Dedicated to

our wives, Georgia and Nancy,
who have journeyed with each of us
for a combined 49 years of marriage.

contents

foreword, Archbishop Demetrios viii

acknowledgments xi

introduction xii

marriage is like a road trip   Session ❶ 1

marriage is a journey...

our purpose today 2

I.   together 3

II. of getting to know each other 9

III. toward oneness 13

IV. of learning to love with God's love 21

V. of being transformed 30

VI. to heaven 31

VII. to heaven 32

sample activity 33

dangers along the way   Session ❷ 35

I.   introduction: GPS for marriage 37

II. first horseman: criticism 47

III. second horseman: contempt 54

IV. third horseman: defensiveness 58

V. fourth horseman: stonewalling 60

couple activity 65

contents

where you've been — Session 3 — 67

   I.   introduction 69
   II. you inherit much more than your genes 70
   III. exploring family of origin 77
   IV. genogram: a family map 78
   George's genogram 79
   couple activity: personal genogram 92
   couple activity: personal genogram questions 94

where you're going — Session 4 — 97

   conversations to have as you
   prepare for your journey 99
   couple activity: a self-examination
   of some important topic areas 104

speaking & listening — Session 5 — 115

   I.   introduction 117
   II. speaking toward oneness 119
   III. listening toward oneness 125
   couple activity 130

contents

packing for the journey   *Session* **6** 133

I.   packing for the journey 134

II.   what can go wrong on a road trip? 136

III. difficulties on your marriage journey 139

IV. couple activity m 141

V.   things to pack 145

VI. marriage is a journey
of acquiring the Holy Spirit 155

final activity 156

Appendices   159

I.   finding help 160

II.   a brief summary of
the sacrament of marriage 165

III. recommended readings 181

about the authors 184

notes...notes...notes...

Beloved in Christ,

I extend to you my warmest congratulations for your engagement and for the love and commitment that you share. The blessings of marriage are abundant, offered by God as you live in relationship with Him and with one another in faith and love.

Also, I commend your commitment to the Sacrament of Marriage within the Orthodox Church and to marriage preparation. Marriage is a sacred bond between husband and wife and is a spiritual relationship that relates to all aspects of life and being. The value and purpose of marriage as ordained by God is affirmed by the Church through this Sacrament. This is also why the Church emphasizes preparation for marriage.

You are making a lifelong commitment to one another and to God in a world that is very challenging. Life itself presents significant issues, but in the midst of all, your marriage relationship should be a source of strength, faith, and even refuge as you share in both joys and struggle. This is the purpose of this resource, *The Journey of Marriage in the Orthodox Church*, and of the sessions you will be attending with your parish priest.

The workbook has been prepared with your needs and hopes in mind, and with a goal of introducing and discussing critical issues that you will be facing in your life together. I encourage you to read and discuss it together and to share your thoughts and questions with your parish priest. I also hope that you will discovor the tremendous value that a marriage preparation has for you as a couple. Your commitment to each other and your journey in marriage is a major life decision, and our goal with this resource and marriage preparation is to strengthen that commitment. A strong and healthy marriage will bless you in so many ways, and it will also lead you closer to God and His will for your lives.

I offer my sincere wishes and prayers for you as you begin this journey together. As you live and love in the bonds of marriage, our good and gracious God will give you guidance and wisdom, and His love will protect you and lead you together to the blessings and promises of life now and for all eternity.

With paternal love in Christ,

†DEMETRIOS
Archbishop of America

acknowledgments

Numerous individuals contributed to the completion of this workbook, many of whom deserve special acknowledgment.

First and foremost, we are especially grateful for His Eminence Archbishop Demetrios' pastoral guidance that permitted and promoted this work. The support of His Eminence Metropolitan Methodios, whose vision for assisting couples preparing for marriage dates back over 25 years, was indispensable in piloting the seminars. The help we received from Frs. Athanasios Demos and Theodore Barbas, Chancellors of the Boston Metropolis, also proved to be of critical importance. Our graphic artist, Chrisanthy Karis, deserves special acknowledgment. Her numerous suggestions, infinite patience, and keen artistic intuitions have had a decidedly positive impact on the look and feel of this workbook. Kerry Pappas and Marilyn Rouvelas also deserve special thanks for the many hours of editing and continued encouragement they contributed. In alphabetical order, we sincerely thank the following individuals for their excellent editorial insights and suggestions: Rosemary Hendrix, Nancy Joanides, and Georgia Mamalakis. Gratitude is also extended to the following priests who agreed to host a premarital education workshop during the piloting process: Frs. Demetrios Kangelaris, Frank Marangos, James Moulketis, Luke Melackrinos, James Moskovites, Demetrios Recachinas and Elias Villis. We are very grateful for the many students at Holy Cross School of Theology who offered their input and assistance in developing this program, particularly Aaron Friar, Lydia Bryant and Alison Hicks. And finally, while it is impossible to list all 350 couples who participated in one of our workshops during the research and development phase, it should be noted that their feedback was of critical importance to the success and development of this program and resource.

We are indebted to *Leadership 100* for their generous financial support of this project.

Philip Mamalakis, Ph.D., LMFT
Rev. Fr. Charles Joanides, Ph.D., LMFT

introduction

So, you're engaged...

many blessed congratulations!

As you must know by now, modern weddings can be stressful events. Making certain that an endless list of concerns are carefully considered and that everything fits together to ensure your wedding day becomes a memorable, joyous event is no easy task. But take heart, with very few exceptions, most couples not only successfully live to tell about this process, they actually have many wonderful memories to share.

But what happens after the wedding and honeymoon are over, and you've begun settling into a process that seeks to blend two separate lives together under one roof? Have you thought much about what it will take to transition from a single to a married lifestyle?

If you've done some thinking about life after the honeymoon and you have some doubts and concerns, please don't be too worried. Doubts and concerns are part of the territory, and most engaged and newlywed couples have them. Then again, if you haven't thought about life after the honeymoon, we would respectfully suggest it's time you do. In either case, we think the workshop you'll be attending, together with the workbook you're reading, can help.

After the Wedding

It's no secret that we live in a divorce culture. Research suggests that more than 40% of all first marriages and 60% of second marriages fail, and that a sizable number (50%) of these failures occur in the first three to seven years. As a result, the Greek Orthodox Archdiocese (GOA), together with your Metropolis and local church in which you plan to marry, require couples planning to marry in the GOA to attend some form of premarital education. That's because the GOA wants to do whatever it can to ensure that couples are not only adequately prepared on their wedding day, but that they're also prepared to take their first steps as husband and wife.

The workshop you'll be attending, together with the companion workbook you'll be using during, and hopefully after, the workshop, are examples of the GOA's concern for all marriages, but especially those who marry in a Greek Orthodox Church. They're intended to prepare you for your marriage journey after the wedding. The priest who will be conducting the Sacrament will explain the preparation process for the wedding. So, if you have questions about the wedding ceremony, consult the officiating priest. However, if you have questions about your journey after the wedding, the workshop and workbook are intended to help you address these questions.

Some Discomfort & Many Insights

By the way, if you're worried about what you'll encounter during this education process, don't be too concerned. The presentations and couple and group exercises are not intended to exclude anyone from marrying in the GOA, nor are they intended to make anyone feel excessively uncomfortable. However, some of the material will challenge both of you to think more carefully about what's needed to ensure that the oneness you're currently blessed with is protected and increases. So, while most of you may experience some moments of mild discomfort, the discomfort will be minimal in comparison to the information and personal and couple insights you'll gain to help you journey together after the wedding.

Six Sessions, Lots of Information, Blessings & Insights

Before you attend the all day workshop, we thought we'd provide you with a thumbnail sketch of the information you can expect to encounter. We hope this short overview will ease your fears and encourage you to take full advantage of this experience. Based on comments from questionnaires that several hundred couples filled out during the research and development of this project, we believe the time and effort you expend will prove worthwhile to you during the transition period from a single lifestyle to a married lifestyle.

For example, Karen in New York has stated, "Great experience...this should be a requirement before people get married." Tom in Boston stated, "I wasn't happy about having to do this, but now I'm really glad I came...a fantastic experience!" And finally, George and Jennifer from Connecticut stated, "The day was filled with lots of great insights and blessings...thank you so much."

Session ① Marriage is like a journey...a journey we decide to take together. This session will present this journey from an Orthodox Christian perspective. Together with the other sessions that follow, our hope is that this session will broaden and enrich your perspective of marriage and family from a Christ-centered perspective, while also helping you understand how your faith background can have a decidedly positive impact on your marital journey together.

Session ② Most couples today begin their journey together as soul mates, and as time passes they end up resembling roommates. A significant number may even begin feeling like cell mates within just a few short years. The reasons why are now well understood. That being the case, in this session we plan to introduce you to a very slippery slope that includes many failed and flawed strategies that couples adopt to deal with their differences, difficulties, and disappointments. Through an understanding of this material, you should be in a better position to detect the warning signs that pull couples toward marital meltdown and divorce and do something about them before things get worse.

Session ③ Your perspective of marriage and family life has been significantly shaped by the family in which you were raised—your family of origin. As a result, Session 3 will be devoted to helping you explore the ways your family of origin has had an impact on your personal perspective of marriage and family life. With your workshop facilitator's assistance, each of you will learn how to create a simple genogram (a family map) of your family background. Once you've completed this exercise, you'll both begin exploring the ways your backgrounds have helped shape your perspective of marriage and family life. You'll also begin to understand the perspectives about marriage and family that you've acquired from your family back-ground that might impact your mutual efforts to cultivate and promote oneness throughout your marital journey.

Session ④ Communication, problem solving, finances, parenting, in-laws, sex, inter-Christian challenges, friends, personal time and couple time are all potential problem areas that can compromise oneness. As a result, during this session you and your future spouse will participate in a self-investigation exercise consisting of a series of 90 questions that are associated with these problem areas. After separately answering these questions and comparing your responses with your future spouse, you should both have a better understanding of (1) your strengths and weaknesses in these areas and (2) where more conversation is needed.

Session ⑤ It's no secret that good communication and listening skills, together with effective conflict resolution skills, are of fundamental importance to marital oneness as you journey together. As a result, this session will provide some useful information that should help you become more effective speakers and listeners. This session will also afford you and your future spouse some practice time to help you begin trying out the skills and suggestions presented. A group wrap-up will conclude this session.

Session ⑥ We believe that the lower divorce rates and higher levels of marital satisfaction that Christ-centered couples report are associated with the timeless treasures and strategies that are embedded within our Holy Christian tradition. Through an explanation of the Orthodox Sacrament of Marriage you will gain a deeper understanding of how a life in Christ can help you negotiate your way around the road hazards, potholes, unexpected detours, and slippery slopes that are part and parcel of every couple's journey together.

Expect to be Exhausted

By the time you complete these six sessions, expect to be exhausted. That's because this day will require lots of hard work. But, here's the good news: along with the fatigue, you should also feel invigorated and more confident about the journey that lies ahead—to God's glory and to your salvation. As John from New York City stated, "It was a long day, and I'm tired. But it was also a good day I won't soon forget." Sophia from Springfield also observed, "Yeah, I'm tired, but I also feel better about what's ahead."

Some Final Suggestions

At this point we hope we've persuaded you to put some quality time into the workshop and its companion workbook. To help you get the most out of these resources, we'd also like to offer a few final suggestions.

① The best way to go through the information in this resource is with your partner and with other engaged couples. As a result, you'll be doing everything together and with other couples like yourselves. By the way, with regard to this last point, you might be interested to know that couples who report high levels of marital satisfaction also indicate that they've adopted a teamwork approach that requires both partners' involvement.

② As you'll hear numerous times throughout the workshop, marriage is like a journey you take together. So, if you don't finish everything, or even understand everything, just remember that you'll be able to go back to the workbook to complete or review what you either did not finish or did not understand on the day of the workshop. Our hope is that you will.

③ As many of you might already know, there's never enough time to get everything done in one day. Well, that was the case as we developed this workshop. As a result, we decided to do the next best thing and provide some suggested readings in Appendix III. After the workshop, we encourage you to continue learning and reading. We suspect this will make all the difference in your efforts to protect and cultivate oneness.

④ We also suspect that if you decide from now to put some quality time into the workshop, couple exercises, group exercises, and the postworkshop suggested readings, you'll be better prepared to begin your journey together. So, here's one last promise. Based on the best research and what we know about the value of premarital education, we believe that if you and your future spouse embrace this process in an effort to get as much as you can out of it, you'll be better prepared to begin your marital journey together—to God's glory and to your salvation.

A Few Final Thoughts

On behalf of His Eminence Archbishop Demetrios, the hierarch who oversees the Direct Archdiocesan District or Metropolis in which you'll be getting married, the priest who will conduct the Sacrament, and your workshop facilitator, blessed congratulations once again; and may the

Grace of the Lord Jesus Christ and the
Love of God
and the fellowship
of the Holy Spirit
be with you."

II Corinthians 13:14

notes···notes···notes···

notes...notes...notes...

marriage is a journey...

marriage is like a road trip • • •

a cross-country road trip that
you decide to go on with someone.

Road trips can be either good or bad experiences.

- What makes for a good road trip?
- What makes for a bad or miserable road trip?

the Journey of Marriage • Session 1

Our purpose today is to...

- introduce you to the **Journey of Marriage** as we understand it in **the Orthodox Church**
    - What it's for
    - What it's like

- clear up any misconceptions or false ideas

- discuss how best to prepare for marriage

- enjoy ourselves along the way

Most couples spend more time preparing for their wedding, which lasts one day, than for their marriage, which lasts a lifetime.

the Journey of Marriage · Session **1**

"What therefore God has joined together, let not man put asunder."
Matthew 19:6

 marriage is a journey **together...**

A. Marriage, like a good road trip, is something the two of you, not others, decide to go on…together.

You will be each other's greatest support, helpmate, and friend.

B. The Church does not support anyone or anything coming between the two of you as a couple.

What types of things can come between a husband and a wife?

_____   _____

_____   _____

_____   _____

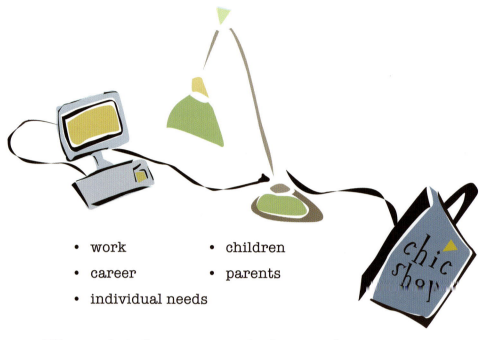

- work
- career
- individual needs
- children
- parents

Who needs to be your top priority on this road trip/journey?

Your: 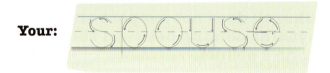 spouse

On this journey, your top priority must be your spouse.

While parents, relatives, and friends are great blessings, your loyalties need to shift.

You need to make your spouse your top priority.

How does this apply to children and stepchildren?

Like parents, relatives, and friends, children and stepchildren are great blessings.

Children may join you on this journey of marriage, and stepchildren might predate the marriage, but they will grow up and leave to begin their own journeys.

Children should come out of marriage—not between it.

So...the best gift you can give your children is a strong marriage.

Research shows that children do better academically, socially, psychologically and spiritually...when the parents have a strong marriage.

C.   Marriage is a journey...together

during the **exciting**...

and

the **monotonous** times.

On a road trip, we have exciting times and see beautiful things, like • • •

• • • • **the ocean**

• • • **the mountains**

• • • **the Grand Canyon**

The exciting times are more beautiful in real life than how people describe them to you.

the Journey of Marriage · Session 1

This is like the journey of marriage.

On the journey of marriage you will have times of excitement when things seem beautiful...

- the honeymoon
- sharing life with another person
- sharing in the joy of children
- quiet dinners together
- the list is endless...

However, cross-country road trips can get monotonous...

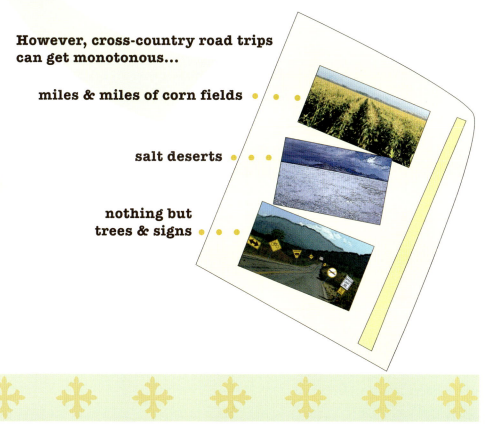

    miles & miles of corn fields

    salt deserts

    nothing but trees & signs

This is like the journey of marriage.

On the journey of marriage you will also experience monotony...

- doing dishes
- changing diapers
- washing laundry
- paying the bills
- the list can seem endless...

What makes the exciting times even more enjoyable and the monotonous times bearable? **Going through them together!**

the Journey of Marriage · Session

II. marriage is a journey of getting to know each other…

A. Marriage is a journey of getting to know your…

- strengths and weaknesses
- dreams and hopes
- values
- likes and dislikes
- quirks and tendencies
- the list is endless…

> "And the man and his wife were both naked and were not ashamed."
> Genesis 2:25

B. Marriage is a journey of getting to know your differences…

Early in your relationship you will focus on similarities. As you continue on the journey of marriage, you will discover differences. You will have different…

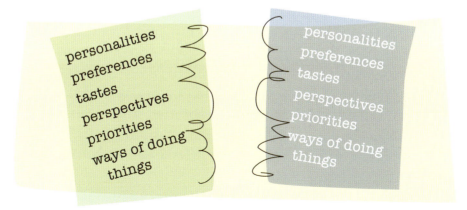

- personalities
- preferences
- tastes
- perspectives
- priorities
- ways of doing things

- personalities
- preferences
- tastes
- perspectives
- priorities
- ways of doing things

ONE PERSON MIGHT...   **and the OTHER PERSON...**

be a night owl ...   an early riser

like things tidy...   doesn't mind stepping over things

be an extrovert...   more of an introvert

believe that early is on time...   operates more on "Greek" time

consider your marriage to be just between the two of you...   consider the extended family as part of the marriage

C. Marriage is a journey of getting to know yourselves

- not only will you learn more about how your partner thinks, feels, and reacts...

- you will also learn more about yourself, and how you think, feel, and react...

- you are going to learn that you have some real strengths, or abilities, and...

the Journey of Marriage · Session 1

You are going to discover that you have some real weaknesses or difficulties with...

- anger
- money management
- sexual relations
- your parents/your in-laws
- depression, anxiety, or other mental illness
- intimacy

Each of you will make these self-discoveries. You can only discover these things in a deeply intimate relationship.

D. Marriage is a journey of getting to know your difficulties...

This process is normal. In your marriage you will discover faults in yourself and in your partner.

- This does not mean that your marriage is fatally flawed or that you married the wrong person.
- What it does mean is that you **need** to attend to these difficulties right away.

Research indicates that couples who divorce have nine areas of major difficulties.

Couples who are successfully married also have nine areas of major difficulties.

Successfully married couples attend to these difficulties.

Couples in failed marriages do not attend to these difficulties.

John's & Becky's First Birthdays Together

Becky always loved surprise parties. She was excited to throw one for John for his birthday during the first year of their marriage. John, for his part, loved to have quiet, intimate dinners for his birthday. When Becky threw him a huge surprise birthday party, with all their friends, John responded, a bit unenthused, "That was nice."

• • •

John decided to show Becky what a real birthday celebration was like when her birthday came around. He found a nice, quiet restaurant and carefully picked out a table for two by the window, overlooking downtown. During the delicious dinner, when he toasted her birthday, he asked her what she thought. She replied, unenthusiastically, "This is nice."

John and Becky are discovering that they have different ideas about how to celebrate birthdays.

the Journey of Marriage · Session

God's purpose is that
a husband and wife become one.

III marriage is a journey   **toward oneness...**

*"For this reason a man shall leave his father and mother
and be joined to his wife, and the two shall become one flesh."*
Matthew 19:5

Marriage is not just about...

- traveling together
- learning more about each other and yourself

Marriage is also about growing closer *toward* one another—becoming one.

"O Master,
stretch out
your hand
from your holy
dwelling place
and join your servants;

for by you
is woman
joined to man.
Yoke them in
oneness of mind;
crown them into one flesh."

Wedding prayer before the Crowning

A. What does oneness mean?

Here are some thoughts to help you understand what oneness means...

- thinking in terms of we, rather than me
- working together as a team, rather than on your own
- working together through the differences, difficulties or disagreements

Is this an example of oneness?

the Christmas Bonus

Christina comes home with her Christmas bonus and announces to Josh, her husband, "Look what I got for my bonus! I've decided to use it as a down payment for a new car."

Josh listens to her and then suggests, "Don't you think we should put it into our savings?"

Christina replies, "I don't think so. This is my bonus, and I'm going to spend it the way I want to."

They are silent for the rest of the evening.

The temptation is to think in terms of me, rather than we...

- his or her towels
- his or her money
- his or her problem

Oneness means to think in terms of *our* towels, *our* money, *our* problems, *our* parents, *our* children, *our* careers...

the Journey of Marriage · Session 1

Oneness means bringing two worlds together to create *our* world. This means...

- getting to know your spouse's world...

    his/her expectations, feelings, hopes, dreams, disappointments, struggles, problems...

- sharing your world with your spouse...

    your expectations, feelings, hopes, dreams, disappointments, struggles, problems...

In marriage, your spouse's feelings, hopes, and struggles are as important as your own.

In marriage 1 + 1 = 1.

 You do not become two halves when you come together as one in marriage because each person is important in coming together to create one life together in Christ.

15

Is this an example of oneness?

> ### Babysitting
>
> Despina announces to Steve that she has figured out who will watch their daughter when they're away on the cruise. "She'll stay with my parents the whole time. My mom said she'd love to do that."
>
> Steve replies, "My mom's been asking to take care of her for months; and I thought we agreed that she could watch her sometime."
>
> "Well," Despina replies, "it's all set. I already told my mom, and that is what we're going to do."
>
> They fight about it for two hours and get nowhere...

D. **Oneness means working together as a team, rather than on your own**

- becoming one mind with your spouse
    - learning to listen to your spouse's thoughts, opinions, priorities, and ideas
    - learning to share your own thoughts, opinions, priorities, and ideas with your spouse
- making decisions together, rather than doing things the way you think is best or right

the Journey of Marriage · Session 1

Is this an example of oneness?

the New Position

Mark came home to report to Julie, "I've accepted the new position at work. I'm so excited. Of course, I'll be working Saturdays now, but my boss says that this is a great opportunity."

"Did you forget that I'm taking a class on Saturdays this fall?" Julie exclaims. "You said that you were going to be around to watch the kids."

"Yeah," Mark replied, "but that was before this job opportunity came up. "Plus...I never really thought that class was a good idea."

Mark thinks the conversation is finished. Julie does not.

- Oneness is like a three-legged race...

- working together as one, getting in step with your spouse
- taking the time to find out what your spouse thinks
- not moving forward until you have both mutually agreed on a plan
- what *we* decide is more important than what *I* think is best

Is this an example of oneness?

Baseball Tickets

Tom calls Shelley, who's pregnant with their second child. "I just got a ticket to the game tonight! If they win, they're going to the World Series."

"Honey, there's no way! I'm not feeling well," she says. "I need you home tonight to watch Johnny."

"I can't pass up this ticket!" he thinks.

C. oneness means...working together through differences, difficulties, and disagreements, rather than working apart or against each other, or on your own...

- putting your spouse's need before your desires
- focusing more on caring for your spouse rather than getting your own way
- understanding the challenges and sacrifices of marriage as opportunities for building oneness

oneness means that the two of you are on this journey together...

- you shouldn't look like a caravan of two cars, instead...

one of you is driving while...  the other is looking at the map

D. oneness is...something you work toward

If you try to row two rowboats next to each other across a lake, the boats are naturally pushed apart. It takes effort to keep them together. That's what oneness in marriage is like.

Oneness...

- takes effort
- takes attention and intention
- takes sacrifice
- takes time and learning

E. oneness is...a gift from God

- Oneness is something you work toward, yet it's a gift from God.
- God makes oneness happen as you learn to love each other...
    - the way He loves (with Christlike love)
    - with His love

†

"Love is patient and kind;
love is not jealous or boastful;
it is not arrogant or rude.
Love does not insist on its own way;
it is not irritable or resentful;
it does not rejoice at wrong,
but rejoices in the right.
Love bears all things,
  believes all things,
    hopes all things,
      endures all things."

I Corinthians 13:4-7

the Journey of Marriage · Session 1

"Marriage is the key that opens the door to discover...perfect love."
St. Gregory Nazianzus

IV. marriage is a journey of learning to love with God's love...

"May the God of steadfastness and encouragement grant you to live in such harmony with one another, in accord with Christ Jesus."
Romans 15:5

God's purpose for marriage
is to teach you how to love each other
like He loves,
with His perfect love,
through the...

- differences
- difficulties
- disagreements

John's & Becky's Second Birthdays Together   continued...

After one year of marriage, John and Becky have gotten to know more about each other and what it means to love someone who often thinks differently.

When John's birthday came around during their second year of marriage, Becky arranged a quiet dinner for just the two of them at a nice restaurant at a corner table, just the way he liked it. While Becky did not think the evening was particularly exciting, John smiled during dinner and shared with her how much her planning and the evening meant to him.

When Becky's birthday came around, John secretly called Becky's friends and organized a surprise birthday party for her—just the way she liked it. While John would not choose this for his birthday, at the end of the evening Becky shared with him how much his planning and the evening meant to her.

John and Becky learn that love means respecting your spouse's preferences even if they are different from your own.

the Journey of Marriage · Session 1

the Christmas Bonus   continued...

After a few days, Josh brings up the Christmas bonus again. "I'm really concerned about how we're approaching our finances."

Christina isn't interested in talking about it. Josh doesn't get angry, but he doesn't forget it. A week later, he brings it up again. "Christina, I think we have a problem. Maybe we need some help." Christina appears to soften, and she says, "Ok, Josh, what do you want to talk about?"

The two of them spend the evening talking about how they want to work together on their finances.

**God's love is expressed as...
a deep commitment
to care for and to serve your spouse...**

God's love is expressed as...

respectfulness ...no matter what
you're feeling.

kindness
gentleness & patience ...rather than anger
criticism, or blame

focusing on what is best
for the two of you ...rather than what you
want for yourself

the Journey of Marriage · Session **1**

With God's love...you can handle your differences

It's easy to love someone who is thinking and feeling just like you are. Marriage is a journey of learning to love your spouse even when you're thinking and feeling differently.

Baseball Tickets continued...

After thinking about it, Tom called up his friend. "I can't go tonight."

"You're kidding. You have to come!"

"No, I can't. Shelley needs me."

He spent the evening taking care of his two-year old and letting Shelley sleep. He watched the game on TV.

"Love one another with brotherly affection; outdo one another in showing honor." Romans 12:10

God's love is...

- sacrificial
- selfless

Marriage forces you to choose between doing what you want and serving your spouse.
Loving your spouse means putting your spouse's needs before your own desires.

Babysitting continued...

The next day, after things calmed down, Steve asked, "Can we talk? I got mad because I felt like you left me out of the decision about who should babysit when we go on the cruise."

"I was frustrated because I worked so hard," Despina explained. "I didn't know it meant so much to you."

"Sometimes I feel like my mom gets left out," Steve added.

Despina replied, "I'm sorry that I didn't check in with you. Why don't you call your mom and see when she's available?"

"I'm sorry for yelling," Steve said. "I'll call my mom today."

the Journey of Marriage · Session 1

Petitions of the Betrothal Service

For the servants of God,
(bride's name) and (groom's name),
who now pledge themselves to one another,
and for their salvation, let us pray to the Lord.

That there may be sent upon them
peaceful and perfect love, and protection,
let us pray to the Lord.

That they may be preserved in concord
and in faith that is steadfast,
let us pray to the Lord.

That they may be blessed with harmony
and perfect trust, let us pray to the Lord.

That they may be preserved in a way
and manner of life that is blameless and pure,
let us pray to the Lord.

That the Lord may grant unto them an honorable
marriage and preserve their marriage bed in purity,
let us pray to the Lord.

translated by Fr. Peter Chamberas
This Is a Great Mystery: Christian Marriage in the Orthodox Church
(Metropolis of Boston: Brookline, MA 2003)

With God's love, you can handle your difficulties

Marriage is a journey of learning to love your spouse, as you discover the faults.

everyone loves the front side of a puppy...

it's hard to love the back side

God's love is... healing

Marriage is a journey of healing your own imperfections by learning to love your spouse, imperfections and all.

- As you seek to love your spouse as Christ loves, you open yourself up to receive God's love.

- As you open your heart, you are healed of your own imperfections—selfishness, impatience, anger, and resentment.

In marriage we are to treat each other "...with all lowliness and meekness, with patience, forebearing one another in love." Ephesians 4:2

the Journey of Marriage · Session **1**

Through this process, you become the person God created you to be...more patient, more selfless, more kind, more gentle, and more loving.

- In the differences, difficulties, and disagreements of marriage, God gives you a choice...

   You can follow Christ and learn to love your spouse like God loves

   or

   You can follow your own reactions and desires.

---

the New Position   continued...

Julie arranged a quiet time to talk to Mark about his decision to take the new position. Initially, he was resistant to even discussing the issue.

Mark shared that he was overwhelmed with everything going on and was worried about being responsible for the kids. They discussed their struggles with working together and decided to go talk to someone about it.

Mark apologized for going back on his agreement. On Monday, he told his boss that he would be free on Saturdays in six months, and if it was still available he could take the new position then.

"Husbands, love your wives, just as Christ also loved the church and gave Himself up for her." Ephesians 5:25

> "If we love one another, God abides in us,
> and His love is perfected in us."
> I John 4:12

V marriage is a journey of being transformed...

God's love in your marriage changes you...

- as you journey together...
- as you get to know each other...
- as you build oneness...
- as you learn to love through the daily challenges of married life...

God's love in your marriage makes you perfect—perfectly selfless and caring toward your spouse. This is what we mean when we call marriage a sacrament. Imagine what type of marriage a couple will have if, over the years, each of them becomes more kind, more gentle, more caring, and more selfless.

the Journey of Marriage · Session 1

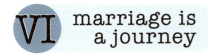

VI. marriage is a journey to heaven...

> "And so marriage is a road:
> it starts out from the earth and ends in heaven."
> Aimilianos of Simonopetra

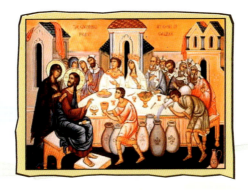

Marriage
does not end in this lifetime

The perfecting
that happens in marriage
prepares us to live eternally with God

The destination of the marriage journey
is heaven

The perfecting
that happens in marriage
is what we call...
salvation

> "Marriage is a sacrament because in it and through it the kingdom of God becomes a living experience."
> John Meyendorff · Marriage: An Orthodox Perspective

VII marriage is a journey to salvation...

"Make [God's] love your aim." 1 Corinthians 14:1

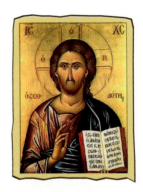

It's through...

- the daily activities of married life
- the exciting and monotonous times
- the daily journey toward oneness with each other
- the learning how to love through the differences, difficulties and disagreements
- the learning to love each other with God's love

that you will experience the "happily ever after" that God desires for each of us.

> "Two people come to the communion of marriage to help one another in their salvation." Monk Moses

COUPLE ACTIVITY

Please take five minutes apart to answer these questions; then come together for 15 minutes to discuss your responses.

1. What, would you say, is the purpose of your marriage?

2. What is God's purpose for marriage?

3. How does your perspective of marriage differ from God's perspective?

4. In what ways are you and your future spouse working toward oneness?

5. What role does checking in with each other play in marriage?

6. What are some of the things that make it difficult to work as one with your future spouse?

7. How do you want to love your future spouse and be loved by your future spouse?

8. In what ways is God's love different from feelings?

9. What makes it difficult to love as God loves?

SESSION 1

notes...notes...notes...

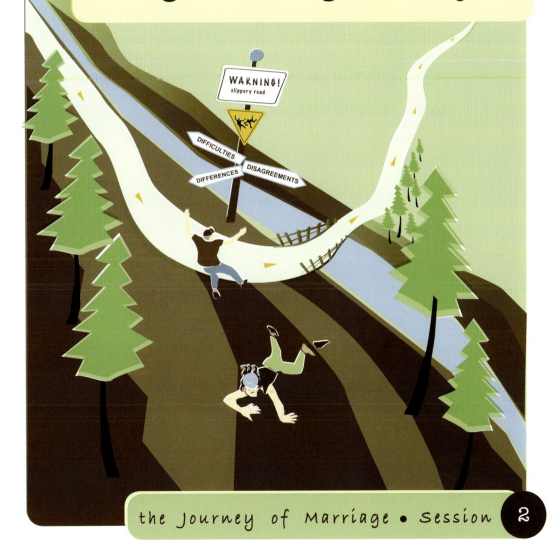

the Journey of Marriage · Session 2

 introduction

GPS for Marriage

In this session, we introduce you to a kind of GPS for marriage—which means that you'll have some valuable information to help you navigate along the journey of marriage—with all the detours, potholes and surprises that you'll encounter along your way.

A. the path toward oneness...review

Session 1 alluded to the path toward heaven. We called it "A Journey to Salvation." It looks like this:

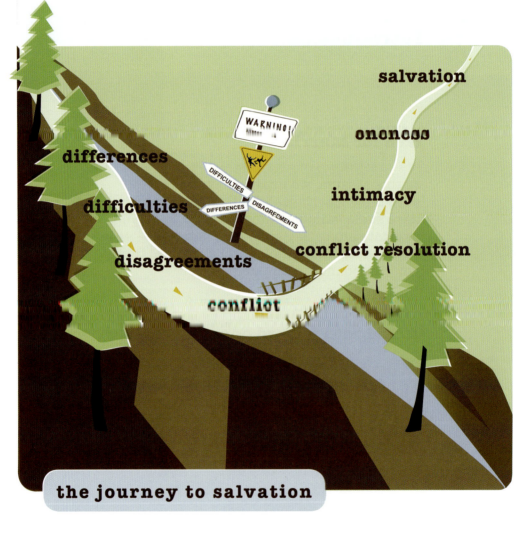

Differences, difficulties, and disagreements lead to conflict, which can lead to intimacy, oneness, and salvation as couples respond constructively.

B. the slippery slope

**...but along the way, there will be a fork in the road
...and you will have a choice to walk toward oneness
...or follow a second path**

Let's take a closer look at this second path.

We are going to look at some of Dr. John Gottman's[*] work. In particular, we are going to look at what he calls...

"the Four Horsemen of the Apocalypse,"
a reference from the Book of Revelation

[*] John Gottman is a well-known marital researcher

In the Book of Revelation Saint John the Theologian
uses the image of the Four Horsemen to signal
the beginning of the end of time:

"...a **white** horse
...its rider had a bow,
and a crown was given to him,
and he went out
conquering and to conquer
...and out came another horse,
bright **red**;
its rider was permitted
to take peace from the earth,
so that men should slay one another;
...and I saw,
and behold, a **black** horse,
and its rider
had a balance in his hand;
...I saw,
and behold, a **pale** horse,
and its rider's mane was Death,
and Hades followed him."

Revelation 6:2-8

the Journey of Marriage · Session 2

Dr. John Gottman uses this image of the Four Horsemen as a sign that a marriage is moving toward meltdown and divorce. When these Four Horsemen begin to appear in your marriage, they signal the beginning of the end.

The Four Horsemen are:

① **criticism**

② **contempt**

③ **defensiveness**

④ **stonewalling**

Viktor Vasnetsov, *The Four Horsemen of The Apocalpse*, 1887, oil on canvas.

41

When couples leave conflicts unresolved, the Four Horsemen appear: criticism, contempt, defensiveness, and stonewalling. This leads to decreased marriage satisfaction, meltdown, and, ultimately, divorce.

O Lord our God, through Your plan of salvation,

You have declared and confirmed marriage to be honorable by Your presence in Cana of Galilee.

Do You Yourself now, O Lord, preserve in peace and concord Your servants, whom You have willed to be joined together in marriage by Your blessing.

Reveal their marriage to be honorable.

Preserve their conjugal life in purity.

Bless their married life to be without any stain of sin, and to remain in faithful chastity.

Make them worthy, O Lord, to reach a ripe old age together and to keep Your commandments with a pure heart.

Service of the Crowning

translated by Fr. Peter Chamberas
This Is a Great Mystery: Christian Marriage in the Orthodox Church
(Metropolis of Boston: Brookline, MA 2003)

B. dangerous curves ahead...

Anyone not attentive to his or her marriage can end up slip-sliding down this path. How can we make this claim? Well... consider the following statistics.

We live in a culture of divorce...

40-50%	of all marriages end in divorce
30%	of all couples report being unhappy
50%	of all divorces occur during the first seven years
45%	of first marriages will not see their 25th anniversary
40%	of all children will grow up without one biological parent in the home

What these statistics imply...

- Many couples who begin their marriage hoping to journey on the right track end up sliding down this slippery slope.

- It's easy for couples to find themselves on this wrong path.

- So...preparing for marriage means learning how to spot the dangers that indicate you are going down the wrong path in marriage.

- You don't want to become one of those statistics!

> O God, our God, who were present in Cana of Galilee and who blessed marriage there, bless also these Your servants who, by Your providence, have now been united in the community of marriage.
>
> Bless them as they go in and out of their home, and fill their life with everything that is good.
>
> Prayer at the removal of the Crowns,
> Service of the Crowning
>
> translated by Fr. Peter Chamberas
> *This is a Great Mystery: Christian Marriage in the Orthodox Church*
> (Metropolis of Boston: Brookline, MA 2003)

If...couples make the wrong choices when they get to that fork in the road...the First Horseman appears on the slippery slope.

the Journey of Marriage · Session 2

II First Horseman

1st Horseman : criticism

There are two types of criticism:
- constructive criticism
- destructive criticism

...which means that not all criticism is bad

A. Constructive Criticism

- focuses on the issue or the problem

Following are two examples:

Bill & Maria two months after the honeymoon:

Bill's Dirty Socks

Bill and Maria are getting comfortable with each other, and they're starting to fall into their old habits, which they had before their marriage.

Bill starts leaving his socks lying on the floor.

Maria starts picking them up—like she thinks a good wife should; but after the fifth or so time, it starts getting old. She needs to do something more than simply picking up after him. So she says, "Bill, let's talk…I like a clean bedroom. Would you mind picking up your dirty socks?"

Bill, now realizing that it bothers her, says, "Sorry, I didn't realize I did that. I'll pick them up. I promise to do better."

And he does do better.

the Journey of Marriage · Session 2

one month later:

Maria & Greek Time

Maria seems to always be on Greek time.

Bill likes to be on time. At first he is patient, but after Maria is late several times, he decides to address the issue. He says, "Maria, let's talk...When you're late, that really bothers me. It's important to me that we are on time. I'd really appreciate it if you'd try and be on time."

And Maria, in response says, "I'm sorry, I'll try to do better."

And...she does do better.

✱ For those who might not know, Greek time is about 30 minutes late.

In both instances Bill and Maria use constructive criticism which...

- focuses on the issue, not the person...
    - Bill's dirty socks
    - Maria's tardiness

B. Destructive Criticism...

- focuses on the person
- loses sight of the issue
- is a direct attack on the person

Here's what it typically includes...

- insults
- mild sarcasm
- name-calling
- impatience

the Journey of Marriage · Session 2

Here is what happens when Bill and Maria choose destructive criticism. The First Horseman enters the relationship.

Bill's Socks — one month later:

Bill and Maria have their morning routine. He gets up early and makes the coffee while she showers. Then they share a quiet cup of coffee together before they head off on their day.

Well, this morning, as Maria steps out of the shower, she sees Bill's dirty socks again on the floor.

"Bill!" she yells, impatiently, "You promised to pick up after yourself!" [impatience]

"C'mon, you can't be that dense." [insult]

"What's so hard about picking up your smelly, dirty socks?" [sarcasm]

That's the end of their "conversation."

Bad habits develop...
and we're not just talking about dirty socks. We're talking about the bad habit of using destructive criticism.

Maria & Greek Time

Maria is upstairs, still getting ready for a 7:30 PM movie. It is 7:20 PM, and it takes 20 minutes to get to the theater.

Bill is stewing as he waits.

Maria makes her way down the stairs as if nothing is wrong.

Bill says, "Uh, I notice that you have a watch on. Have you ever thought about looking at it once in a while?" [sarcasm]

"You've made us late again!" [blame, impatience]

They argue, and stay mad. Imagine how the date goes.

They don't talk about it anymore.

More bad habits develop.

We're not just talking about...

how couples handle dirty socks and tardiness! We're talking about choices—how couples have a choice about how they address their differences and difficulties... either constructively or destructively.

We could easily be talking about other things like...

- joint or separate checking accounts
- replacing the toilet paper roll
- getting/forgetting milk from the store

the Journey of Marriage · Session

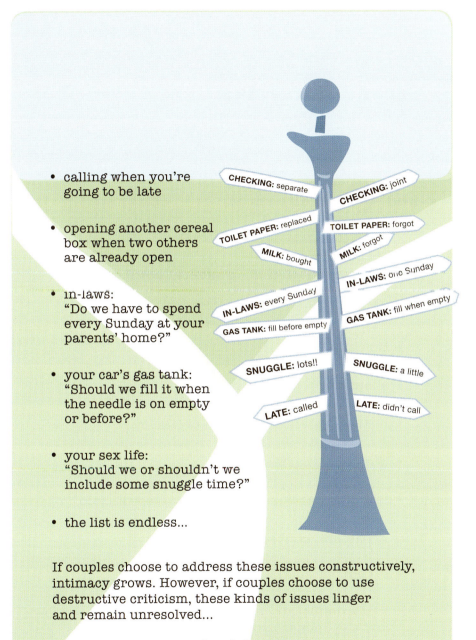

- calling when you're going to be late

- opening another cereal box when two others are already open

- in-laws:
"Do we have to spend every Sunday at your parents' home?"

- your car's gas tank:
"Should we fill it when the needle is on empty or before?"

- your sex life:
"Should we or shouldn't we include some snuggle time?"

- the list is endless...

CHECKING: separate / CHECKING: joint
TOILET PAPER: replaced / TOILET PAPER: forgot
MILK: bought / MILK: forgot
IN-LAWS: every Sunday / IN-LAWS: one Sunday
GAS TANK: fill before empty / GAS TANK: fill when empty
SNUGGLE: lots!! / SNUGGLE: a little
LATE: called / LATE: didn't call

If couples choose to address these issues constructively, intimacy grows. However, if couples choose to use destructive criticism, these kinds of issues linger and remain unresolved...

and couples slide down
the slippery slope toward the...

Second Horseman

What is contempt?
It's criticism ratcheted up several notches!

- biting insults

- threats

- shouting

- liberal amounts of hateful profanity

- hurtful sarcasm

- lots of impatience and destructive criticism

Like criticism, contempt is toxic! Why?

- It gets personal!

- It is a deliberate, hurtful attack on the other person and the oneness you desire to build.

- It hurts!

- Contempt is filled with...

    - anger
    - resentment
    - revenge
    - meanness

Let's look at what happens when contempt enters a relationship.

Bill & Maria   six months later...

> **Note:** This is 11 months into Bill and Maria's marriage, and look what's happened.

Maria comes home from work. Murphy's Law is in effect all day for her. Everything that can go wrong did go wrong.

Bill is also exhausted, sitting in the recliner, channel surfing and decompressing.

Maria passes him with barely a glance. Bill grunts as Maria heads to the bedroom to change. And guess what she finds on the floor? She grabs the dirty socks, furious, and heads back to Bill in the TV room. She stands in front of their HD TV, waving the socks and says...

"Bill, you are such a #@! jerk!" [profanity, name-calling]

"I'm done picking up after you!" [threats]

"You're so selfish!" [insult, contempt]

Then she throws the socks at Bill and leaves.

They don't talk the whole night and most of the next day.

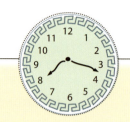

Maria & Greek Time   continued...

Maria's car needs some work, so Bill agrees to let Maria use his car, as long as she picks him up after work on time. She agrees and promises to be on time.

It's 5 o'clock, and Maria has not arrived. She arrives at 5:30 pm. Bill has been standing out in the rain without an umbrella, stewing and becoming increasingly upset.

Maria pulls up and, before she even has a chance to say hi, he lays into her.

"Where the !@#$ have you been? You can be so !@#$ selfish!" [profanity, insult]

"Sometimes I think we'd be better off divorced!" [threat]

"I'm so sick and tired of you always..."

Before he has a chance to finish his attack, she drives off.

Bill ends up taking a cab home.

They don't speak for days!

the Journey of Marriage · Session 2

They keep sliding down the slope...

- Notice how quickly a couple can slide into contempt.

- If enough criticism and contempt enter into a couple's exchanges, the Third Horseman soon arrives...

IV Third Horseman

3rd Horseman : defensiveness

Defensiveness...

is your effort to protect yourself from an attack and from being hurt.

Defensiveness...

builds up a wall between you and your partner in order to protect yourself.

Defensiveness...

blocks connection and undermines oneness.

The same wall that couples put up to protect themselves blocks intimacy.

the Journey of Marriage · Session 2

Here is what defensiveness sounds like eighteen months after the wedding...

> Maria: "You're such a pathetic slob!"
>
> Bill reacts: "Yeah, and you're Ms. Perfect!"
>
> Bill: "You can never be on time!"
>
> Maria: "I'm not always late."
>
> Bill: "And it's not my fault."
>
> Maria: "Yes it is! You started it!"
>
> Bill: "Yeah, yeah, it's always my fault!"

People become defensive ...

- when they feel attacked.
- to protect themselves from more hurtful attacks.
- and point fingers of blame to deflect their partner's criticisms and contempt.

After enough criticism, contempt, and defensiveness enter a couple's arguments, the Fourth Horseman appears...

Fourth Horseman

Stonewalling: when a person shuts down, shuts up, tunes out, and turns away from the other...

Why do spouses stonewall?

- They're worn down and tired of arguing about the same things in the same hurtful way.

- They're flooded with negativity, like anger, resentment, rage, hurt and shame.

- They're sick of being attacked and don't know how to respond—or don't want to respond anymore—for fear of what they might say or do. So...they shut up, shut down, tune out, and turn away from one another.

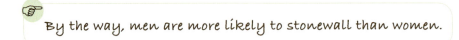

By the way, men are more likely to stonewall than women.

the Journey of Marriage · Session 2

> "Have no anxiety about anything,
> but in everything by prayer and supplication
> with thanksgiving let your requests be made known to God."
> Philippians 4:6

Bill & Maria sliding out of control...

24 months into their marriage, Bill is shutting down more regularly.

In response, Maria is becoming more resentful and angry. Bill stonewalls even more.

At this point, they're not able to effectively talk to each other about practically anything, let alone what they're really struggling with.

They are sliding down...out of control.

- Men and women have just as many feelings.
- In general, women are different from men in the way they experience emotions and in their ability to manage them effectively.
- Generally, men have more difficulty managing their emotions than women.

> "Rejoice in your hope, be patient in tribulation, be constant in prayer."
> Romans 12:12

If these Four Horsemen hang around long enough, guess what happens?

- instead of oneness, two different worlds emerge...

Many couples who get caught on this slippery slope...

- begin as soul mates
- turn into roommates
- end up feeling like cell mates

the Journey of Marriage · Session 2

> "For this very reason make every effort to supplement your faith with virtue, and virtue with knowledge, and knowledge with self-control, and self-control with steadfastness, and steadfastness with godliness, and godliness with brotherly affection, and brotherly affection with love."
>
> 2 Peter 1:5-7

Bill & Maria continued...

As Bill continues to stonewall, eventually Maria is going to give up.

When that happens, the couple disconnects, making it increasingly difficult to come back together again.

Intimacy has been lost.

Trust is gone.

Friendship is lost.

Hurt, resentment, and anger have built up and are filling their relationship.

The marriage has melted down, and divorce is imminent.

It is at this time that couples are susceptible to infidelity.

As the marriage melts down, the relationships at work seem more attractive.

If marriage is like a road trip, then Bill and Maria are a wreck on the side of the road.

So...please remember this!

- In this divorce society, all marriages are vulnerable.

- Bill and Maria ended up— in a very short time—at the bottom of that slippery slope.

- They had a lot of choices along the way, but were not attentive to the warning signs.

- Marriage is a journey of oneness, which, if you choose, leads toward intimacy and happiness.

- But if you choose the wrong path, you will end up at the bottom of that slippery slope.

So, when you see one of the Horsemen appear in your marriage, attend to your spouse and marriage on your journey together.

- Make your spouse a top priority.

- Make oneness a top priority.

- Guard against the Four Horsemen.

- Beware of the slippery slope...so you don't end up a statistic.

COUPLE ACTIVITY

Please take five minutes apart to answer these questions; then come together for 15 minutes to discuss your responses.

1. Who/what are the Four Horsemen?

2. Which one of these guys is most likely to hang around your relationship?

3. What makes it so easy to slip-slide down the slippery slope?

4. What place do insults, name-calling, sarcasm, profanity, and impatience play in a marriage?

5. What effect will blaming, criticizing, selfishness, or thinking only about yourself have on your future marriage/spouse?

6. When are you most likely to slip-up with your future spouse?

7. What are better ways to respond to your future spouse at those times?

8. What information shared in Session 1 can help you stay off the slippery slope?

9. What are some examples of some little things that might infect your marriage with negativity and distance?

SESSION 2

notes...notes...notes...

where you've been...

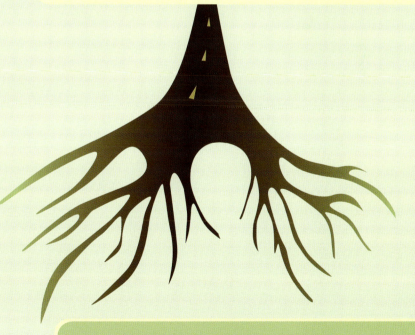

the Journey of Marriage • Session 3

the Journey of Marriage · Session 3

introduction

To prepare for marriage you need to learn what marriage is for (Session 1) and what marriage is like (Session 2). You also need to know as much about each other as possible, which we will do in Session 3 and Session 4.

You may have noticed as you've gotten to know your future spouse that he/she is a lot like his/her parents. Why is that? It's because...

II you inherit...

much more than your genes from your parents.

A. You inherit a way of being in the world.

> **Your families shape...**
> - the way you see the world
> - the way you act
> - the way you think
> - what you value
> - our ideas about God and the Church
>
> The list is endless of the ways the families in which we grew up shape how we are in the world.

the Journey of Marriage · Session 3

For example, let's take a look at another couple.

Meet Brittany & Kosta

Kosta loves sports. His dad played semi-pro baseball when he was young, and Kosta played baseball in college. He fondly remembers his dad being at baseball practice with him (often on Sunday mornings), going to baseball games, and watching baseball on television together. Kosta's family went to church only on Christmas and Easter. Brittany's family was actively involved in their church community. Brittany thinks that Sundays don't feel like Sundays unless you go to church. Most children's sports teams play their games on Sunday mornings.

 When should Brittany and Kosta have a discussion about sports, church, and Sunday mornings?

B. You inherit a way of understanding love.

Your families shape...

- how you love

- what you expect from love

- how you express love

- how you relate to others

- how you treat people and how you expect to be treated by people

- how you show respect, affection, and even how you argue

- the list is endless...

Our families not only shape how we understand the world, but also how we understand love.

the Journey of Marriage · Session 3

Meet Peter & Cindy

Peter grew up in a home with five brothers. Family members often teased one another and engaged in passionate discussions. When Peter has a strong opinion about something, he tends to raise his voice. In fact, it is not uncommon for Peter to get into "heated discussions" with his brothers when they see one another.

Cindy was an only child and rarely saw her parents get angry. She prefers to quietly discuss things. She feels hurt when Peter teases her and scared when he raises his voice. While growing up in her family, people only yelled when things were really out of control.

 When should Peter and Cindy discuss how to express themselves to each other?

It's clear that the best time to discuss these issues is before the wedding.

C. You inherit expectations about marriage.

Your families shape your assumptions and expectations about what family life should look like...

- how to be a husband or wife
- what to expect from your husband or wife
- how to communicate
- how to work together
- how to resolve conflict
- the list is endless...

The families in which we grew up shape our expectations about the world, about love, and about marriage and family life.

the Journey of Marriage · Session 3

Meet George & Amanda

George's mom has taken care of the household his entire life. He's never seen his father help in the kitchen, clean the house, or help with the children. George's dad ran the family business and made all the major decisions. His mom never wrote a check and never learned to drive.

Amanda and her brother rotated chores, and her father would cook every other day. Amanda's mom has several CD recordings and teaches music theory at the local junior college. She also handles all the finances in their home.

 When should George and Amanda discuss household roles and responsibilities?

Despite what you've learned about marriage from TV, the movies, books, or from your friends, the home in which you grew up has the greatest influence on what you believe and expect about marriage and family.

notes...notes...notes...

III exploring family of origin

One of the best ways to get to know yourself and your future spouse is to explore, together, the families you grew up in and how you've been influenced by them.

Exploring your families is **not** about deciding who's right and who's wrong.

- It's about...
    - getting to know yourself and each other
    - deciding, together, how you will do things in your new family
    - building oneness

Creating your own family...

- While you had very little to say about how your parents ran their home, you have a lot to say about how you and your future spouse run your home.

- This type of mutual effort establishes healthy patterns for working together on your journey of marriage.

- Exploring your families together builds oneness and helps the two of you decide openly how to set up your own home.

IV genogram: a family map

In this session, we're going to take time to explore the families in which you grew up and work together to decide how the two of you would like to run your new home.

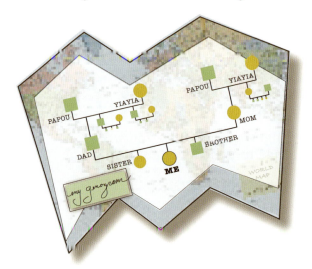

Exploring your family...

- To explore your family, you are going to use what's called a genogram.

- A genogram is like a family map, or a family tree, that contains a lot of information about how your family functioned.

the Journey of Marriage · Session 3

We're going to learn how to draw a genogram by creating a family map of a young man named George. Let's draw George's genogram.

GEORGE'S GENOGRAM

George is a male—indicated by the square, with his age, 25, written in the square and his name below. Females are depicted by a circle.

```
   ┌────┐
   │ 25 │
   └────┘
   GEORGE

ACCOUNTING DEGREE
WORK VERY IMPORTANT
DOES NOT WANT KIDS
AVOIDS CONFLICT
```

George has a younger brother, 23 years old.
Siblings are depicted oldest to youngest from left to right coming down from the parents' marriage line.

George has two parents.
His dad is 46 and his mom is 44.

What do you notice about his parents?
His parents married in 1979 and divorced in 1985.
The solid line connecting George's mom and dad indicates a marriage. The divorce is indicated by the slash lines.

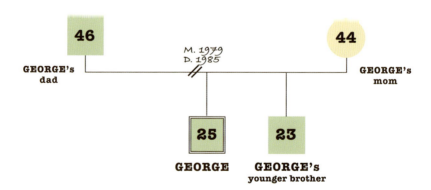

Who are the family members of George's mother?
His mom has two parents—
a father, age 76, and a mother, age 68.

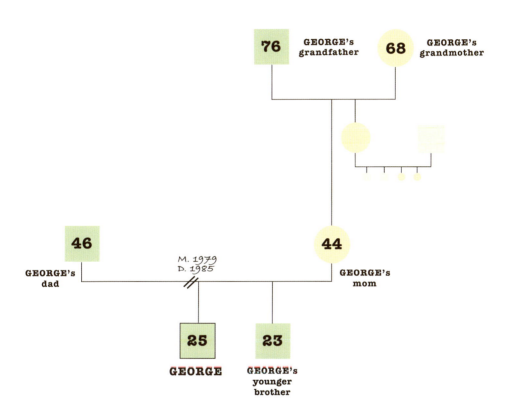

Mom is the oldest of two girls.
Her younger sister is married with four children.

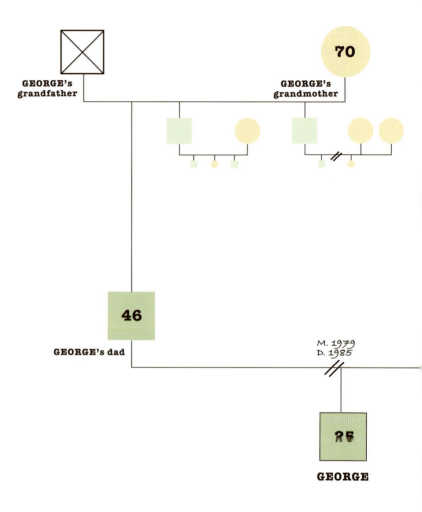

George's paternal grandfather is deceased.
This is indicated by an X in the square.
George's grandmother is 70.
George's dad is the oldest of how many children?
He is the oldest of three boys.

the Journey of Marriage · Session 3

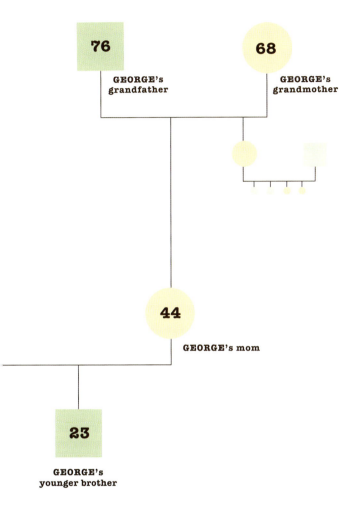

George's dad:
Notice that George's dad has a younger brother who is married with three children. His youngest brother was married and had two children, then divorced and remarried. Notice how this remarriage is depicted. These are George's two uncles.

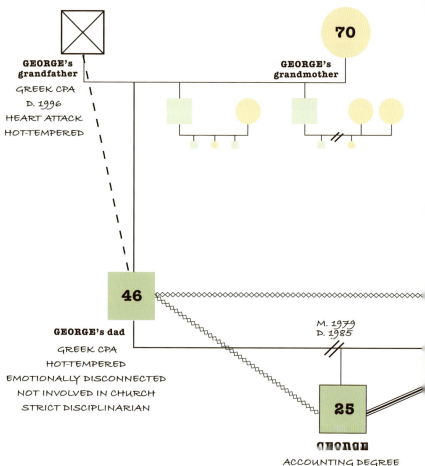

> The first step in creating a genogram is mapping out the structure of the family—at least three generations.
>
> Then you will fill in some information about each of the significant people in the genogram. You write what each person does professionally, each person's ethnic and cultural background,

the Journey of Marriage · Session

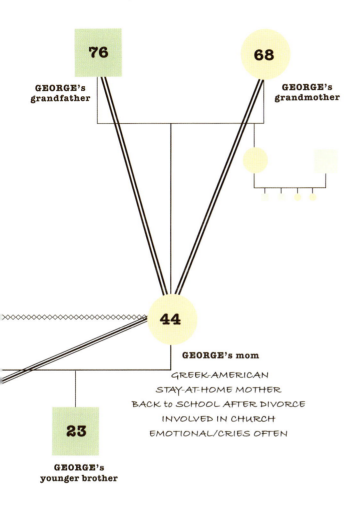

religious background, and any significant medical or physical illnesses. You indicate in the genogram any significant life events that have occurred—like war, immigration, or major accidents.

Then you indicate any important personality traits for each significant person in the genogram.

- **George has an accounting degree.** His work is very important to him. He does not think he wants any children and avoids conflict. *Where does George get these traits?*

- **George's dad was born in Greece and he is a CPA.** He is hot-tempered, emotionally disconnected from the family, not involved in church, and a strict disciplinarian.

- **George's mom is a Greek-American and a stay-at-home mom.** She went back to school after the divorce. She is actively involved in the church. She is very emotional and cries often.

The final step in doing a genogram is to describe the significant relationships. You want to show on the diagram how your parents got along, how you got along with your parents and with others in your family. You do this by using different symbols to describe different relationships.

- **The line between George's dad and mom is a high conflict line**, indicating that there was a lot of conflict in that relationship. *How would you describe George's relationship with his dad? ...highly conflictual.*

- **A dashed line indicates a lack of closeness**— as you can see in George's dad's relationship with George's grandfather.

- **A double line indicates a close relationship**— as you can see in George's mom's relationship with her parents. *What do you see between George and his mother? ...very close,* as indicated by the triple line.

the Journey of Marriage · Session 3

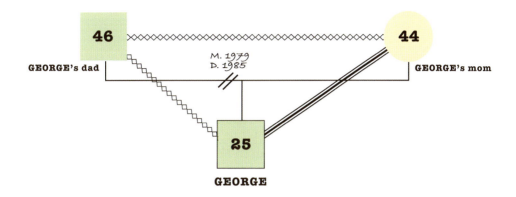

Now that you have completed the genogram, you can look at what issues George might have to discuss with his fiancée.

Looking at family history gives you good information about what things you should pay close attention to in your own life.

This is just like looking into your family's medical history. ***How can you find out if you are at risk for heart disease?*** You can look into your family history of heart disease.

In the same way, exploring the patterns of behavior in your family can give you insight into what you should pay close attention to in your own relationships.

Looking at George's family, what issues might need some special attention?

Anger

George's father was hot-tempered in a marriage with a lot of conflict. George's grandfather was also hot-tempered. George and his fiancée need to have a talk about how they want to handle anger in their relationship.
They might ask questions like...

- Is it OK to get angry?

- When do I tend to get angry?

- What is the best thing to do when I am angry?

George can then discuss how his fiancée's family handled anger as well.

Sadness

For some people, growing up in a home with a very emotional parent results in an intolerance or discomfort with crying.

- Is George's fiancée free to cry?

- How will George respond to his fiancée's emotional expressions?

- How does George express sadness?

- Is George comfortable crying with his fiancée?

Parenting

George's father was a strict disciplinarian and emotionally distant from his children. George has indicated that he does not want any children. George and his fiancée will have to make sure to have a discussion about children, if any, and how many.

- What will George's role be in raising the children?
- Does George want to be involved as a dad, or not?
- Will he continue his father's parenting approach, or is he interested in learning a better approach?

Conflict Resolution

George tends to avoid conflict. Is it possible that George has developed an aversion to conflict because there was so much conflict in his household growing up between his mom and dad?

- What are George's experiences and perceptions about conflict?
- How will George and his fiancée handle conflict when it arises?

It is impossible to avoid conflict in marriage. George needs to discuss, with his fiancée before they are married, how the two of them will resolve the inevitable conflicts that arise in marriage.

Extended Family

George is the oldest son and very close to his mother, who is divorced and lives alone. *What question might come up shortly after the wedding about George's mother? "When is she moving in?"* Because of the closeness of the relationship and his mother's living situation, George and his fiancée need to discuss what role his mother will play in their lives.

- What role should George's mother play in George's decisions with his fiancée?
- Is it OK if George's mother moves in with them after the wedding?

Finances

George, as an accountant, is likely to have specific ideas about how to manage money. It is important that the two of them decide together and are clear about how they will handle their finances.

- How will their money be earned, saved, and spent?
- Who will manage the finances?
- Will they make major financial decisions together, or will George make them by himself?

There are many different ways couples can answer these questions. George and his fiancée need to make sure they have this discussion before they are married.

Notice...The genogram highlights areas that George and his fiancée need to be certain to discuss prior to the wedding.

the Journey of Marriage · Session 3

We would like you to create your own genogram. After you have completed it according to the steps on page 92, answer the questions on pages 94 and 95 and share your answers with your future spouse. The facilitator is available to assist you.

> **Wrap-up questions/comments...**
>
> - What are some things from your own familics that you would liko to oontinuo in your new family?
>
> - What are some things that you'd like to do differently in your new family?

We know that there is not enough time today to finish this exploration of your families.

- We encourage you to continue this exploration and discussion about the families you came from and how to build your new family in the coming months.

- In fact, this is something that needs to continue to happen throughout your journey of marriage as you grow toward oneness.

COUPLE ACTIVITY · PERSONAL GENOGRAM

As you prepare to join with another person to create a new family, you have an opportunity to choose, together with your future spouse, to repeat the way things were done in your family growing up or adopt new ways of doing things.

The following questions are a guide for you as you construct your family genogram on page 93. Once you have completed your genogram, proceed to pages 94 and 95. You have 30 minutes to create your genogram and answer the questions.

1. Draw a genogram of at least three generations on both sides of your family (your mother's and your father's) and include names and ages of all family members. Use the symbols demonstrated by the presenter and noted in the corner of the next page.

2. Indicate who is married, separated, divorced, pregnant, deceased, etc., and include the dates of these significant events in the genogram.

3. Next to each significant person, indicate what that person did/does professionally.

4. Next to each significant person, indicate the person's education level.

5. Next to each significant person, indicate his/her cultural heritage (nationality or ethnicity) and religious affiliation.

6. Next to each significant person indicate any significant physical or mental health illnesses in that person's history (heart attack, cancer, diabetes, depression, etc.).

7. Next to each significant person indicate any significant life events (war, immigration, trauma, major surgery, etc.).

8. Next to each significant person indicate any significant personality traits (hot-tempered, never got mad, very quiet, withdrawn, domineering, passive, always giving, etc.).

9. After you have indicated the facts, using the different relationship lines indicate how your parents got along when you were younger.

10. Indicate any other significant relationship history by putting relationship lines between the significant individuals. If possible, have a line indicating each of the marriages depicted in the genogram as well as between you and your siblings, parents, and significant grandparents. If possible, indicate any significant relationships between your parents and their siblings as well as your siblings.

MAN
WOMAN
DECEASED

MARRIED
DIVORCED
CHILDREN

CLOSE
REALLY CLOSE
NOT CLOSE
CONFLICT/ FIGHTING

COUPLE ACTIVITY • PERSONAL GENOGRAM

Once you have completed the genogram, answer the following questions. Share your genogram and your answers to these questions with your future spouse.

1. How did people get along in your family growing up?
   How did you and your siblings get along?
   Who was close to whom?
   Is there anyone in your family that nobody speaks to?

2. How would you describe your parents' relationship (good, fair, bad, close, distant)?
   How did your parents show affection to each other?

3. How did your parents work through problems?

4. How did your parents make major decisions?

5. What are the most important values in your family (honesty, education, hard work, faith, generosity, etc.)?

6. How did people get along in your family growing up?
   How did your parents divide household duties?
   Who did what, and how did they decide (household
   chores, parenting responsibilities, etc.)?

7. How did your parents discipline you and your siblings?
   How did they show affection to you and your siblings?

8. How did your parents manage their money
   (who earned it, who decided how it was spent,
   who managed it, who paid the bills, etc.)?

9. How did your family spend the holidays?

10. What role will your parents play in your new family?

11. What kind of relationship do you have with your in-laws-to-be?

notes...notes...notes...

where you're going...

the Journey of Marriage • Session 4

the Journey of Marriage · Session 4

 where you're going...

conversations to have as you prepare for your journey...

It's impossible to know everything about your future spouse before you get married. Despite this fact, it's important that you check in with each other before the wedding and carefully consider some potential problem areas. Research indicates that the following problem areas can create distance and undermine oneness:

Problem areas...

- communication
- problem solving
- finances
- parenting
- in-laws
- sex
- ethnic and religious differences
- friends
- personal time versus couple time

It's OK to learn some of the little things about your spouse after you're married; however, what if, after the wedding, you discover that...

YOUR HUSBAND...

YOUR WIFE...

doesn't like to problem solve with you when you have a big decision to make?

likes to spend money, while you prefer to budget and save?

wants his children from his first marriage to call you "Mommy," and you want them to call you by your first name?

wants a career and isn't interested in starting a family, while you were hoping to begin a family soon and have several children?

does not want to baptize your kids, and you were expecting them to be baptized?

In these instances, the "what ifs" might create some problems. The best time to identify and address these issues is before marriage, as you get to know each other better.

the Journey of Marriage · Session 4

Because these problem areas can undermine oneness, or build oneness if they're handled correctly, we are devoting an entire session to them.

DIRECTIONS...

- Each of you will fill out a questionnaire

- This is not a test!

It's a self investigation—a way to help you identify your strengths and potential blind spots!

First Step...

- Fill out the questionnaire on your own.

- Take as much time as you need.

As you're answering the questions...

If a question raises concern, and you would like the two of you to discuss further, check the blank space in front of the question.

For example...

- Under the problems labeled "communication,"

    _____ Our disagreements often
    end in a heated argument, and
    that upsets me.

- If that's something that troubles you, check it.

Second Step...

- Once you're both finished, let the
  conversation begin!

- Go through each item you checked
  and discuss why you checked it.

- We recommend you take turns.

- You'll have about 30 minutes to complete
  Step One and Step Two. If you don't finish...

Third Step...

- Resolve to continue the conversation
  in the coming week.

- Suggestion: Make an appointment with
  each other; otherwise this conversation
  might not continue.

the Journey of Marriage · Session **4**

If you do this correctly...

- You'll find yourselves entering into a respectful, learning experience, one that will...

    - help connect the two of you

    - facilitate "oneness"

    - put good patterns in place for how to work together on your journey of marriage

What if...

- Some serious concerns emerge?

    Take time to talk about these issues with each other!

What if...

- Lots of serious concerns emerge?

    Consider getting some outside help!

CONVERSATIONS TO HAVE AS YOU JOURNEY TOGETHER...

A self-examination of some important topic areas
If unable to complete Step One and Step Two in 30 minutes,
finish discussing together in the coming week.

I. Communication

1. ____ I wonder if my family's way of communicating has affected my style of communication.

2. ____ I believe our communication skills need some improvement.

3. ____ I don't think my future spouse always listens to what I have to say.

4. ____ My future spouse sometimes thinks I don't listen to him/her.

5. ____ After we've argued, our differences often remain unresolved.

6. ____ Our disagreements usually end in a heated argument, and this upsets me.

7. ____ There are some things I don't feel comfortable talking about with my future spouse.

8. ____ There are some issues that we can't discuss.

9. ____ I find it difficult to say "I'm sorry," even when I'm wrong.

10. ____ I can't always turn to my future spouse for emotional support.

11. ____ I believe our faith in Christ can help us improve our communication.

II. Problem Solving

12. _____I'm afraid of my future spouse's temper.

13. _____ I'm concerned about my future spouse's temper.

14. _____ My future spouse has resorted to physical and/or verbal violence when we've argued.

15. _____ I've resorted to physical and/or verbal violence when we've argued.

16. _____ I don't think I can disagree with my future spouse on some topics.

17. _____ We don't seem to reach many mutually satisfying resolutions.

18. _____ I would like to change the way we resolve problems.

19. _____ My future spouse always wins our arguments.

20. _____ I like to always win our arguments.

21. _____ I'm concerned about my future spouse's silent treatment.

22. _____ My future spouse makes me feel bad when we disagree.

III. Finances

23. ____ I wonder if our different family backgrounds related to finances might cause problems.

24. ____ I think we need to talk more about how we will manage our money.

25. ____ I have some concerns about my future spouse's spending habits.

26.____ I don't believe we've talked enough about the money and the debts that we are bringing into our marriage.

27.____ I wonder if my future spouse will feel inadequate if I make more money than him/her.

28. ____ I still think we need to talk more about our future financial security.

29. ____ I believe we need to talk more about credit cards.

30. ____ I wonder if we have a Christ-centered perspective regarding our finances.

IV. Parenting

31. ____ I wonder how our family backgrounds will affect our efforts to parent our future children.

32. ____ I wonder how my future spouse feels about having children.

33. ____ We need to talk more about how many children we want.

34. ____ We need to talk more about when we will start a family.

35. _____ We need to talk more about the parenting strategies we will use.

36. _____ We need to talk more about how we will discipline our future children.

37. _____ We need to talk more about how our role as parents will not become more important than our marriage.

38. _____ I have concerns about my future spouse's children from a previous marriage.

39. _____ I wonder if we have a Christ-centered perspective regarding parenting.

V. Sexuality

40. _____ I wonder how my family's attitudes toward sex might affect our sex life.

41. _____ I want a strong sexual relationship with my future spouse, but I don't know if my future spouse feels the same way.

42. _____ I feel uncomfortable discussing sex with my future spouse.

43. _____ Some of my future spouse's attitudes about sex trouble me.

44. _____ I still think we haven't talked enough about contraception.

45. _____ I wonder how our past sexual activities might impact our sex life.

46. _____ I may be uncomfortable around my future spouse when I'm nude.

47. _____ I wonder how a Christ-centered perspective regarding sex can help.

VI. In-Laws

48. _____ I have some difficulty accepting or feeling comfortable around my future spouse's family.

49. _____ I think my future spouse might be having difficulty accepting or feeling comfortable with my family.

50. _____ I believe our different religious and ethnic backgrounds may cause some problems.

51. _____ My family hasn't given us their blessing to marry, and I wonder how significant this will be.

52. _____ I don't feel entirely accepted by my future spouse's family.

53. _____ In-laws continue to interfere with our wedding plans, and we don't know what to do about it.

54. _____ Rather than siding with me, sometimes my future spouse sides with his/her family.

55. _____ I'm concerned that our families will expect too much of our time.

56. _____ I wonder if our marriage will be less important than extended family responsibilities.

VII. Inter-Christian Challenges

(If both future spouses are Greek Orthodox, you may skip to the next section.)

57. _____ We've agreed about where we will worship.

58. _____ We've agreed about where we will pledge, and the amount of our pledge(s).

59. _____ I still feel as though I have questions regarding my future spouse's faith tradition.

60. _____ We still need to talk more about where the children will be baptized.

61. _____ I feel uncomfortable in my future spouse's church.

62. _____ I disagree with some of the traditions and beliefs that are part of my future spouse's faith tradition and wonder if this will affect our oneness.

63. _____ We haven't talked enough about our ethnic and cultural differences.

64. _____ I'm concerned because I don't believe we've talked enough about our religious differences.

65. _____ I've wanted to bring up the topic of conversion, but I am hesitant because I don't want to disrespect my future spouse.

VIII. Friends

66. _____ My future spouse's friends make me uncomfortable.

67. _____ My friends make my future spouse uncomfortable.

68. _____ I'm concerned that my future spouse may spend too much time with his/her friends after marriage.

69. _____ We don't seem to have many friends in common.

IX. Personal Time vs. Couple Time

70. _____ I am concerned that my future spouse won't respect my desire to cultivate personal hobbies and interests.

71. _____ I think my future spouse spends too much time watching television, surfing the net, or playing video games.

72. _____ Some of my future spouse's interests and hobbies concern me.

73. _____ Our interests are very different, and this concerns me.

74. _____ Our ideas regarding vacations seem to be very different.

75. _____ My future spouse tends to make all the decisions regarding vacations.

X. Second Marriage

(If neither of you have been previously married, please skip to the next section.)

76. _____ I wonder if a previous spouse will create problems for us.

77. _____ I don't believe we've talked enough about child support and alimony payments.

78. _____ I wonder if my future spouse's children will come first.

79. _____ I wonder if my future spouse thinks his/her children will come first.

80. _____ I wonder if I've talked enough to my children about my decision to remarry.

81. _____ I'm not sure about the role I will have in the lives of my future spouse's children.

XI. Miscellaneous Concerns

82. _____ My hope is that marriage will change some of my future spouse's habits.

83. _____ I sometimes wonder if I'm ready to get married.

84. _____ There are some things about my future spouse's personality that irritate me.

85. _____ I sometimes wonder if my future spouse wants to change certain things about me.

86. ____ I wonder if my future spouse has a drug or alcohol problem.

87. ____ I wonder if my future spouse will support my career goals.

88. ____ My future spouse tends to have a very traditional view of marriage, and this sometimes concerns me.

89. ____ We haven't talked enough about household chores.

90. ____ We haven't talked enough about gender roles.

When both you and your partner have finished, respectfully discuss your answers together. Remember to work as a team. Be respectful and don't be too concerned if you don't reach full consensus.

If you do this exercise correctly, you'll identify many of your strengths and some of your potential vulnerabilities.

notes ⋯ notes ⋯ notes ⋯

notes...notes...notes...

speaking · listening ... & the journey of marriage

the journey of Marriage · Session 5

the Journey of Marriage · Session 5

 introduction

Ladies, have you ever been driving somewhere together and gotten scared because of how fast your fiancé is driving?

What do you say when you get scared because of the speed?

"You're going too fast!"

"Where'd you learn how to drive?"

"You're a reckless driver!"

"Slow down! You're driving too fast!"

What kind of comments are these?

Criticism: ① **The First Horseman**

Gentlemen, what is your response when your fiancée says that you are driving too fast?

"No, I'm not."

What kind of comment is that?
You're defending yourself and your driving, right?
That's...

Defensiveness: **The Third Horseman**

Both of you are now sliding down the slippery slope... and you're still scared about how fast the car is going.

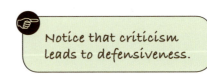

Is there a better way?
Yes... speaking and listening toward oneness.

Notice that criticism leads to defensiveness.

the Journey of Marriage · Session 5

 speaking toward oneness...

**What if you focused on sharing your world—
"I'm scared," rather than criticizing his world
(his driving).**

What would that sound like?

- *"Honey, I'm scared how fast we're driving."*

- *"Honey, I'm not comfortable driving this fast."*

This is speaking toward oneness.

**A. Speaking toward oneness is about...
sharing your world, rather than criticizing
the other's world.**

- *"I'm feeling carsick."*

- *"I'm getting scared from the speed."*

It is the constructive criticism we talked about earlier...

- focusing on the problem, not the person.
- talking about yourself, not your spouse—using "I" statements.

When you use the pronoun "I" rather than "you," you communicate that you are talking about your world and yourself.

- "I am not comfortable with your tone of voice."
- "I really appreciate it when you ask me before making a decision."
- "I am disappointed that you still have not talked to your mother about Christmas vacation."

rather than...

- "Quit yelling."
- "Who died and made you king/queen?"
- "You're afraid to talk to your mother!"

"I" statements help to keep you focused on your own world.

Speaking toward oneness is about offering your whole world to your spouse...

- Your thoughts...

    - *"I don't think we should spend our money like that."*

    - *"I would rather have some time just to be with you, than be with your entire family."*

- Your feelings...

    "I'm scared." "I'm sad." "I'm happy."

B. Speaking toward oneness avoids:

- "you" statements...

    "You never..." "You only..." "You don't..."

- the Four Horsemen

- blame

- emotional reactivity

Speaking toward oneness communicates...

- *"I care about you and your world."*
- *"I value your opinion."*
- *"I value you."*
- *"I love you."*

Here are some examples of speaking toward oneness:

- *"I'm disappointed that you didn't call."*
- *"It hurts me when you criticize my mother."*
- *"I get scared when you raise your voice."*
- *"I feel ignored when you make decisions without me."*
- *"I feel cared for when you call."*
- *"I appreciate it so much when you..."*

As you can see, we are not talking about our driving habits. We are talking about how to respond to every difference, difficulty, and disagreement in daily life.

C. What does speaking toward oneness require?

- **Self-Awareness**
  - You can't share until you are aware of how you're feeling and what you're thinking.
  - Sometimes that means you have to slow yourself down and become more aware of your inner world before you speak.

- **Time**
  - to reflect.
  - to put into words what you feel and what you think.
  - together to share.

It takes time to become aware of and clear about what you feel and think. Rather than sliding down the slippery slope, you need to slow down a little and reflect on what you really feel and think. You need to slow down to share respectfully with each other. This means that you have to resist the temptation to impulsively react, attack, or criticize.

Resisting these temptations requires...

- **Self-Control**

    - to avoid sliding down the slippery slope.

    - to speak with respect as you share your world rather than attack and criticize the other person's actions.

- **Courage**

    - to calm yourself down and try to identify your feelings and thoughts.

    - to discover what might be difficult, sad, scary, or painful to face.

    - to make new discoveries about yourself.

Ladies, if you simply share that you are scared of the way your fiancé is driving, what might your fiancé do? ...ignore, dismiss, criticize, mock— essentially, hurt you.

It takes courage to share what you really feel.

If you decide to share your world rather than attack, you open yourself up to being attacked, dismissed, ignored, or hurt, again. You also open yourself up to becoming closer to each other, but closeness can be refused. Sharing your world takes courage because it makes you vulnerable. Sharing your world with your future spouse is an expression of love.

- **Love**

  - When you open yourselves up to each other, resisting the temptation to attack or criticize, this act of self-control and courage is also an act of selflessness. It is an act of respect and an act of love.

  - Speaking toward oneness takes love and it is an expression of love.

Sharing your world says:

"I love you and I want to grow with you," in the midst of the daily activities of marriage.

the journey of Marriage · Session **5**

 listening toward oneness...

back to the speeding car...

Drivers, what choice do you have when the passenger shares...
"I'm scared how fast you're driving."

The temptation is to ignore, dismiss, criticize, mock, or hurt.

You have a choice between...

selfishness...
dismiss
disregard
criticize
attack

or

oneness...
listening

What's more important, to get there a few minutes early, or to get there connected with your spouse?

What is listening toward oneness?

A. Listening toward oneness...is about paying attention to your spouse's world and making your spouse's world—

- feelings
- thoughts
- ideas

more important that your own...at that moment.

B. Listening toward oneness avoids...

- evaluating, analyzing, blaming, ignoring, mind reading, or even problem solving.
- the Four Horsemen and the slippery slope.
- multitasking (we need to pay attention).
- thinking about how to reply.
- finding problems and shortcomings in what your spouse is saying.

Listening toward oneness communicates...

- "I care about you and your world."
- "I value your opinion."
- "I value you."
- "I love you."

C. What does listening toward oneness require?

- **Silence...**

inside and out

> Inside
>
> - calming yourself down
> - taking a deep breath
> - counting to ten
> - giving yourself a time-out
>
> Outside
>
> - not speaking
> - tracking what your partner is saying
> - being intentionally attentive

"Be joyful in hope, patient in affliction." Romans 12:12

Listening toward oneness requires...

- **Time**
    - to listen to each other and
    - to check in with each other.

The temptation when listening is to react, to interrupt, to answer, to correct, to defend, to criticize, to condemn...

- **Self-control**
    - not to go down the slippery slope.
    - not to react to what someone is saying.
    - not to dismiss them when you don't agree.

It takes real self-control to listen quietly when your future spouse is speaking, so...

- **Selflessness**
    - Listening is about sacrificing yourself, your way, your ideas, your thoughts, your feelings; putting yourself aside in the moment, for your future spouse.
    - It takes real selflessness to allow someone else to speak, particularly when you disagree or when it is hard to listen.
    - It takes real selflessness to resist the temptation to react, so...

"No marriages fail from too much listening." Anonymous

Listening toward oneness requires...

- **Love**
    - When you control yourself and resist the temptation to attack or criticize, this act of self-control—this act of selflessness—is an act of respect and an act of love.
    - Listening toward oneness takes love and it is an expression of love.

Listening to your spouse says:

"I love you, and I want to grow with you," in the midst of the daily activities of marriage.

Dr. John Gottman claims that a couple will have a successful conversation most of the time when the following two things occur:

1. If the wife (who usually brings up topics) has a slow start-up, that is, if she speaks toward oneness, and
2. If the husband attends to what she says, that is, if he listens toward oneness.

Whether you are listening or speaking, in each exchange you have as a married couple, you have a choice between oneness or selfishness. In every exchange you encounter that "fork in the road." It is in the very routine and daily exchanges of married life that God invites you—if you choose—to grow in oneness.

COUPLE ACTIVITY: SPEAKING & LISTENING TOWARD ONENESS

We learn how to speak and listen toward oneness by practicing. Please read through and complete the following activity.

The Speaker-Listener Technique*

Rules for Both of You

1. *The Speaker has the floor.* Use a real object to designate the floor. We're pretty concrete; we have actually given couples pieces of linoleum, so when someone says they have the "floor" they really mean it! You can use anything, though: the TV remote, a pen, a paperback book. The point is that you have to use some specific object, because if you do not have the floor, you are the Listener. As Speaker and Listener, you follow the rules for each role.

2. *Share the floor.* You share the floor over the course of the conversation. The Speaker is the first one to hold the floor. After the Speaker talks, you switch roles and continue, the floor changing hands regularly. This is a trust issue: you trust that you will have the floor when you need it, so you can pass it to your partner when she/he needs it.

3. *No problem solving.* When using this technique, you are going to focus on having a good discussion, not trying to come to solutions. When you focus on solving a problem, you are far less likely to hear what each other thinks about that problem. Your "STUFF" (thoughts, feelings, desires) will distract you from LISTENING. This is your chance to practice putting your STUFF aside and just listen to your partner.

Rules for the Speaker

1. *Speak for yourself.* Don't mind read. Talk about your thoughts, feelings, and concerns, not your perceptions of the Listener's point of view. Try to use "I" statements, and talk about your own point of view and feelings. "I was upset when you forgot our date" is an "I" statement. "I think you don't care about me" is not.

2. *Don't go on and on.* You will have plenty of opportunity to say all you need to. To help the Listener listen actively, it's very important that you keep what you say in manageable pieces. If you are in the habit of delivering monologues, remember that having the floor protects you from interruption. You can afford to pause to be sure your partner understands you.

3. *Stop and let the Listener paraphrase.* After saying a bit, stop and allow the Listener to paraphrase what you just said. If the paraphrase is not quite accurate, you should politely and gently restate what you meant to say in a way that helps your partner understand. This is not a test! You want to make it possible for your partner to understand you as well as she/he can.

Rules for the Listener

1. *Paraphrase what you hear.* You must paraphrase what the Speaker is saying. Briefly repeat back what you heard the Speaker say, using your own words if you like, and make sure you understand what was said. When you take the time to restate what you heard, you show your partner that you are listening. If you truly don't understand some phrase or example, you may ask the Speaker to clarify, but you need to limit yourself to just asking for explanations.

2. *Don't rebut.* Focus on the Speaker's message. While in the Listener role, you may not offer your opinion or thoughts. This is the hardest part of being a good Listener. If you are upset by what your partner says, you need to edit out any response you may want to make and pay attention to what your partner is saying. Wait until you get the floor to make your response. You will have your chance, and when you do, you'll want your partner to extend the same courtesy to you. When you are the Listener, your job is to speak only in the service of understanding your partner. Any words or gestures to show your opinion are not allowed, including making faces!

Flip a coin to determine the first Speaker. The Speaker selects a topic to discuss, possibly one of the items you checked in Session 4. Once the Speaker has decided upon a topic, follow the instructions of the Speaker-Listener Activity.

* from Howard Markman, Scott Stanly, & Susan Blumberg's
Fighting for Your Marriage, 3rd edition, Jossey-Bass Books (2010)

notes....notes....notes....

packing for the journey...

the Journey of Marriage • Session 6

I packing for the journey

Imagine if someone told you he/she was heading on a road trip with a friend, from Boston to California, but wasn't going to pack for the trip.

You ask, *"Why not?"* The person answers, *"We love each other so much that we are sure it will just work out."*

the Journey of Marriage · Session 6

What would you say to the person?

"What do you mean?"
"That doesn't make sense."

- **Being in love and being prepared
  are two different things.**

- **Really wanting to be together is
  different from really being prepared.**

- **Strong emotional attachment is
  not enough for the journey.**

When differences, difficulties, and disagreements
arise, romantic feelings dissipate and are replaced
by frustration, disappointment, criticism, etc.

In fact, if you really want to be together for the whole
journey, the best thing to do is to prepare.

Being prepared is what we've been talking about today.

In this session we're going to introduce you to some
real strategies that need to be in place to help you on
the journey.

what can go wrong on a road trip?

What can go wrong on a road trip?

- flat tire
- accident
- get lost
- run out of gas
- mechanical difficulties
- traffic
- bad weather
- speeding ticket...

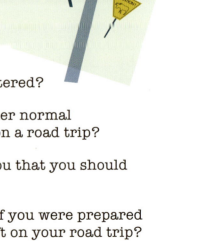

Which mishap have you encountered?

Which mishap would you consider normal or reasonably likely to happen on a road trip?

Which mishap would mean to you that you should not have gone on the road trip?

What difference would it make if you were prepared for these mishaps before you left on your road trip?

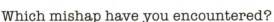

the Journey of Marriage · Session 6

Consider getting a flat tire. What difference would it make if you did not have a spare tire and a tire-jack?

the difference between a minor inconvenience and being stranded.

- Some of these mishaps are out of your control—bad luck.
- Some are caused by mistakes you make.
- Some are caused by inattentiveness.

When mishaps occur on the journey...

- It doesn't mean you should not have gone on the road trip.

- It does mean you should put care into packing.

This is like the journey of marriage.

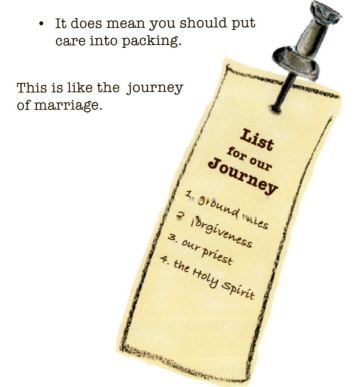

List for our Journey
1. Ground rules
2. forgiveness
3. our priest
4. the Holy Spirit

the Journey of Marriage · Session 6

III difficulties on your marriage journey

On the journey of marriage you will encounter many normal and reasonable difficulties.

- Some will be out of your control:
    - illness
    - losing a job
    - parenting challenges

- Some will be caused by mistakes you make:
    - getting into debt
    - not making your spouse your #1 priority
    - over-committing yourselves

- Some will be caused by not paying attention to your marriage:
    - differences
    - difficulties
    - disagreements

When these difficulties arise...

- it doesn't mean you should not have gotten married.

- it does mean that before you head off on your marriage journey, you need to "bring a few things along with you" so that you are prepared.

the Journey of Marriage · Session ❻

 couple activity...

This activity asks you to do two things:

1. To look at how to help one of the imaginary couples we presented today.

2. To come up with a list of things you think are necessary to "bring along" on the journey of marriage.

Remember Bill and Maria—
with the dirty socks and Greek time?

When we last left them, they were a wreck on the side of the road.

Couple Activity

Bill and Maria are disconnected. They are sliding down the slippery slope towards marital meltdown.

- Answer the questions together in the Couple Activity on the next page, and then partner with another couple and discuss your answers.
- You have 15 minutes.
- Be prepared to share with the group.

COUPLE ACTIVITY

1. What did Maria and Bill each do that slid them down the slippery slope? (see Session Two)

2. What choices do Bill and Maria each have at this time?

Circle the choices that will build oneness and cross out the ones that will slide them farther down the slippery slope. Discuss what you think the best three choices would be.

Leave or quit.

Forgive each other.

Change the way they're speaking toward each other: Speak and listen toward oneness.

Go to talk to someone about their frustrations and pain.

Read a book/attend a seminar on how to work through the difficulty.

Take a time-out.

Say a prayer.

Go talk to their priest.

Consult an attorney.

Keep yelling.

Go criticize their spouses to their parents.

Go talk to friends who don't like the spouse.

Go see a friend who is in the process of divorce.

Check-out and watch television.

Prepare for and receive Holy Communion.

Act like everything is fine, and hope it goes away.

Continue to blame each other.

Don't tell anyone about it. Try to just endure.

Keep doing the same thing, and hope for a different result.

Don't go to a therapist because they don't really have a problem.

Go find some people who will validate his/her own side and demonize the other.

Develop some ground rules for their relationship.

Go to confession.

Look at wedding pictures, and remind themselves of why they got married.

Hitch-hike or find another ride on the journey with someone cute from the office, or an old boyfriend/girlfriend.

Other:_____

3. What can Bill and Maria put in place to avoid slipping down the slippery slope in the future?

SESSION 6

143

Large Group Discussion

Go around the room and share your top three choices for Bill and Maria's answers.

Things to Pack

What would be different if Bill and Maria:

- had ground rules in their relationship?
- knew about forgiveness and confession?
- had a priest with whom they could speak?
- understood the role of the Holy Spirit?

the journey of Marriage · session 6

 things to pack for the journey of marriage...

Consider the following items Bill and Maria could have packed, that each one of us will need on our journey...

- **ground rules**
- **forgiveness**
- **your priest**
- **the Holy Spirit**

145

> *"Be angry and do not sin:*
> *do not let the sun go down on your wrath."*
> Ephesians 4:26

A. Ground Rules

On your wedding day, you are not just getting married; you are beginning your married life together. Marriage is a journey, not a destination. It is an ongoing, daily journey of turning toward each other in response to Christ's command to:

> *"... love the LORD your God*
> *with all your heart, with all your soul,*
> *with all your mind, and with all your strength,*
> *and love your neighbor as yourself."*
> Mark 12:30-31

The moment you take each other for granted and stop checking in with each other is the moment you are at risk for slipping down that slippery slope we discussed.

The best time to "look at a map" and discuss where you want to go and how you want to get there is before you depart. You don't need a map to drive through your hometown, but you do need a map to drive to new towns and to new parts of the country. Marriage is a journey to a new land, to new places. Now is the time to discuss how you want to treat each other, how you want to be treated by each other, how you want to work together, and how you want to love each other.

Couples are most likely to struggle with each other when they have differences, difficulties, and disagreements. Happy couples have specific ground rules to help them work together through these issues.

> *"Let all bitterness, wrath, anger, clamor, and evil speaking*
> *be put away from you, with all malice."* Ephesians 4:31

the Journey of Marriage · Session 6

Consider some of the problem areas you checked in Session Four. When are the two of you most tempted to turn against each other or slip down the slippery slope? Consider what we discussed in Session One about oneness and love, as well as speaking and listening toward oneness in Session Five. Establish some ground rules that you think would be important for you and your future spouse.

Some couples are tempted to turn against each other when they are angry. They need a rule forbidding themselves to yell at each other. Other couples are more likely to become so busy in their individual lives that they slowly drift apart. They need a ground rule about how they will stay connected to each other daily.

Here are some examples of ground rules for relating:

- No destructive criticism, contempt, defensiveness, and stonewalling.

- Never criticize your future spouse to your family.

- Never criticize each other's faults.

- Never yell at each other, unless the house is on fire.

- Call a time-out if discussions get heated.

- Operate as one on all major decisions.

- Share difficult feelings with respect.

- No spending more than 20 dollars without checking in with each other.

- Check in with each other daily.

- Take the time to address the bigger issues.

- Seek first to listen before speaking.

> "Do nothing out of selfish conceit, but with humility of mind let each of you regard one another as more important than himself."
> Philippians 2:3

You show your love for each other by making ground rules and sticking to them no matter how you feel. Developing ground rules together makes you active participants in the journey of marriage; active participants in seeking to love each other.

Your ground rules are the map for your journey that you use to navigate the differences, difficulties, and disagreements that arise in marriage.

Have you ever been driving with a map and still gotten lost?

That is what the journey of marriage is like. You need ground rules for how to relate to each other, but you also need a plan when you break one of the rules.

For that reason, you need to bring something else along on your journey...

the Journey of Marriage · Session **6**

B. Forgiveness and Confession

Everyone fails at some point in his/her marriage. In happy marriages, when you fail, you ask for forgiveness.

Forgiveness is a choice to let go of anger and resentment, while working through the problem, to get back on the path of oneness. Forgiveness is the beginning of the healing process in marriage and the way you grow closer to God. Forgiveness is obedience to God's command.

"For if you forgive others their trespasses,
your heavenly Father will also forgive you,
but if you do not forgive others their trespasses,
neither will your Father forgive your trespasses."
Matthew 6:14-15

Forgiveness is...

- saying you are sorry for something that you have said or done that hurt the other person, no matter what the other person said or did to you.

- admitting you are wrong, you made the wrong choice, and went down the wrong path.

- taking responsibility for your part in sliding down that slippery slope.

- saying, *"I still want to work toward oneness, but I blew it."*

"Blessed is he whose transgression is forgiven, whose sin is covered."
Psalm 21:1

Forgiveness is...

- saying, *"I am not perfect, but I want to learn how to love you with perfect love."*

- being willing to do things in a different way— *"I will not do that again."*

- believing that God's mercy and love are greater than your sins and mistakes.

- saying, *"I love you, but I did not show it."*

Love means always being ready to say you're sorry.

"And be kind to one another, tenderhearted, forgiving each other, just as God, in Christ, also has forgiven you." Ephesians 4:32

Forgiveness is not...

- pretending a mistake was not made. Rather than, *"That's ok; I forgive you,"* you say, *"That was not OK, I forgive you."*

- conditional. Rather than, *"I'll forgive you if...,"* you say, *" I forgive you, and...we need to talk about what happened. We need help working through this, I am still sad or hurt."*

- automatic reconciliation. Sometimes you can forgive but the problem still needs to be addressed before the two of you can come back together again. You say, *"I forgive you, and you need to go talk to someone about your anger/spending/addictive behavior before we can come back together."*

Forgiveness is not...

- forgetting. You will still remember the transgression, and it might still hurt; but when you forgive someone, you remember in a different way, without anger, resentment, or a desire to retaliate.

- impossible. *"I can't forgive you,"* means, *"I am not ready to forgive you,"* or *"I am too hurt to forgive you."* Christ can forgive anything you ask Him to forgive, and He helps you to forgive those who have hurt you.

Forgiveness Rituals

What you will discover in marriage is that if you are serious about learning how to love with Christ-like love, you will struggle, and you will make mistakes. Happy couples practice regular forgiveness.

- Daily, asking each other for forgiveness

- Weekly, before going to church on Sunday, asking each other for forgiveness

Confession

Forgiveness is a gift God gives to get you back on the path of oneness whenever you find yourself slipping down that slippery slope. He gives the gift of forgiveness as you turn toward Him with your mistakes in confession.

God offers confession, through His Church, to wipe away your mistakes, get you back on track, build oneness in marriage, and fill you with His love. Through confession God heals your illnesses that caused you to slip down the slippery slope in the first place.

With forgiveness and confession, God sets you both free from your mistakes and turns you from cell mates back to soul mates!

After you ask each other for forgiveness, you can then ask God for forgiveness through confession. The Sacrament of Confession is practiced by going to talk to your priest about your mistakes and your struggles. The priest stands as a witness as you share your mistakes and struggles with Christ. If you want to practice regular forgiveness and confession, you'll need to bring someone else with you on your journey.

"Therefore confess your sins to one another, and pray for one another, that you may be healed. The prayer of a righteous man has great power in its effects."

James 5:16

C. Your Priest

All couples get stuck once in a while along the journey of marriage. For some couples, the first year of marriage can be the most difficult as they learn how to work together toward oneness.

- Healthy and happy couples get help.

- Your marriage is not just between the two of you.

You will be married in front of a community of friends and family, and when couples get divorced, a community of people is affected.

Couples who think that what happens in their marriage is no one else's business are at risk for getting stuck without any resources to help them get unstuck.

- Bringing a priest along on your journey of marriage is like having AAA roadside assistance on a road trip.

- Bringing a priest along on your marriage will help you keep your marriage on the right path.

- Christ leads couples to stay on the right path.

Bringing a priest, or someone such as a couples' therapist who understands the journey of marriage, who knows the way, and with whom you both feel comfortable, helps you to keep Christ as the guide on your journey of marriage.

God's desire for your marriage is that you acquire His love for your spouse, which is why you need Christ to be the guide of your marriage. This means, also, that you need to bring one more thing on your journey.

D. The Holy Spirit

"And hope does not disappoint, because God's love has been poured out into our hearts through the Holy Spirit which was given to us."
Romans 5:5

The Holy Spirit pours out God's love in marriage. God makes oneness happen through His Holy Spirit. Oneness is something you work toward, but it is the Holy Spirit that makes it happen.

"But the fruit of the Spirit is love, joy, peace, patience, kindness, goodness, faithfulness, gentleness, self-control...." Galatians 5:22-23

It is in and through the Holy Spirit that your love is transformed into divine love. Through the Holy Spirit you participate in the divine love of God. Only the Holy Spirit can give you divine love in the face of the differences, difficulties, and disagreements in marriage, because only God's love is unfailing, unconditional, and unending.

the Journey of Marriage · Session 6

VI marriage is a journey of acquiring the Holy Spirit...

You acquire the Holy Spirit...

- by learning how to pray.

    Praying the Lord's Prayer together, each evening
    Praying before meals
    Worshipping together on Sundays

- by working toward oneness with your spouse daily.

    Working toward oneness opens your heart to receive the Holy Spirit.

- by learning to practice forgiveness and confession.

    By saying, *"I'm sorry,"* you say *"Yes,"* to God's healing.

    Going to confession invites the Holy Spirit into your heart.

- by living your marriage within the life of the Church.

The marriage ceremony takes place in a church, rather than outdoors in a park. Your marriage journey begins in a church and needs to remain within the life of the Church. This journey of marriage is not only about your promise to love each other; it is also about God's promise to send the Holy Spirit with you on your journey. Staying connected to the Church is how we stay connected to the healing that comes from God through the Holy Spirit.

VII final activity

We have presented you with a lot of information to help prepare for marriage. We've talked about the purpose and nature of marriage. We've taken some time to explore the families you come from, what each one of you brings into your marriage. We've explored how speaking and listening in the daily interactions of marriage can move you toward oneness or slide you down the slippery slope. And, we've talked about what you need to pack for the journey.

Our seminar will end today, but your marriage journey is just beginning.

At this time, we'd like to give each of you an opportunity to share. From what we have discussed,

- What is one thing you would like to take with you from this seminar on your journey of marriage?

- *What is one thing you would like to stop doing or leave behind (bad habit, something you'd like to stop doing in your relationship, distorted thought, unrealistic expectations, etc.)?*

Conclusion:

God's plan for marriage is that you live happily ever after. But His way toward happily ever after is learning how to love each other with His love, by inviting Him into your marriage, so that His love is what is guiding your marriage. When God's love guides your journey, your marriage will grow in peace and in happiness, now and forever and to the ages of ages.

†

O merciful God,
we beseech You ever to remind us
that the married state is holy
and that we must keep it so.

Grant us Your Grace
that we may continue
in faithfulness and love.
Increase in us the spirit of
mutual understanding and trust,
that no quarrel or strife
may come between us.

Grant us Your blessings,
that we may stand before the people
and in Your sight as an ideal family.
And by Your mercy,
account us worthy of everlasting life:
for You are our sanctification,
and unto You we ascribe glory,
to the Father
and to the Son
and to the Holy Spirit,
now and forever,
and unto the ages of ages.
Amen

notes...notes...notes...

Appendix I

Finding Help

If you discovered some serious differences you were unable to work through together, we urge you to spend more time attempting to resolve these differences. If this strategy doesn't work, we encourage you to consider getting some outside help. The following information should prove helpful.

Getting Help Is Scary

First off, we realize that this last recommendation may be somewhat intimidating to you because making such a decision could slow down your marriage preparations. It might also cause you to rethink your decision to marry. We can't predict the end result of such an inquiry. However, we can state that the serious, unresolved differences you've discovered won't go away just because you decide to get married. If anything, the probability is that these differences will get bigger and more complex over time, ultimately undermining oneness and marital satisfaction.

So, as scary as it might seem to you to admit you have serious differences that require special attention, the correct and brave decision isn't to ignore them but to address them before marriage. The bottom line is this: as intimidating as it may seem to consider outside help at this juncture, the family court system in our country is littered with couples who ignored serious warning signs and blindly proceeded forward with marriage only to regret such a decision in the aftermath a year or two later.

Couples' Therapist

Finding the help you need may be easier said than done. As a result, our first suggestion is that you make an appointment with your priest. He may be willing to provide some counseling or help you find some suitable help. Either way, we strongly suggest you begin your search by consulting your priest. If your priest is unable to help, follow these additional suggestions.

We have no doubt that there are some very good couples' therapists in your area. The challenge for you, however, is finding them. That's because the average person has little knowledge of the mental health field. Turning to the Internet, Yellow Pages, or even a provider list that your insurance company offers is no guarantee you'll find the help you need. You may get lucky, but you might also end up selecting the wrong therapist whose approach could do more harm than good.

- The first consideration you should keep in mind in your search for the right therapist is to choose with care. Don't be in a rush. If you put in the time on the front end of this search process, your efforts to find a good fit should pay dividends on the back end of this process.

- Word of mouth is often a good way to start your search.

- Doing an online search for a couples' therapist can prove profitable. The following Web sites are good places to begin your search: www.aamft.org, www.marriagefriendlytherapists.com, and/or www. aapc.org. These sites have therapist locators that can help you identify the best couples' therapists in your area. These sites also provide profiles of each therapist that describe their work and expertise. Reading these over will help you get an idea of how they approach their work.

- As you're searching, look for a therapist who has extensive experience working with couples. Two credentials you should look for are a Licensed Marital and Family Therapist (LMFT) and a clinical member of the American Association of Marital and Family Therapists (AAMFT).

- Once you've developed an initial listing of three or four therapists, you will want to begin calling to make an initial connection. Here are some questions you might consider asking: Do you have any openings? What percentage of your work is with couples? What percentage of the couples with whom you work are engaged or dating couples? Do you use one of the following premarital questionnaires: FOCUS, PREPARE, RELATE, or PMI? (These are the best promarital preparation inventories. If a given therapist isn't familiar with these instruments or doesn't use one of them, we would suggest you continue looking.)

- Some therapists will have more time to answer your questions than others. If a therapist hasn't any time and prefers to simply make an appointment, we would recommend you continue looking. Conversely, you also shouldn't expect the therapist to spend more than five-ten minutes with you. If your initial impressions are favorable, we would suggest you consider setting up a consultation with the therapist to learn more about his/her work.

- During the consultation session, you will want to ask how the therapist works, as well as what success rate he or she has in helping couples remain together. You'll also want to ask the following question: Do you seek, primarily, to promote personal growth or marital well-being? Some therapists place more value on individual well-being and personal growth than they do on promoting marital well-being. So, if you are interested in improving your relationship, choose someone who will help you accomplish this objective. Otherwise, you may find yourselves quickly moving in a direction you hadn't expected.

- Be aware that couples' therapy can be costly and that most insurance plans do not cover this type of therapy. However, when you compare couples' therapy with attorneys' fees and future court appearances, the cost is minimal by comparison.

- While most people don't want to appear "difficult," there is a fine line between being difficult and respectfully assertive when hiring a therapist. If you remember that you're seeking to build a team that will assist you and your partner in making some important changes and decisions, this strategy may help you be respectfully assertive.

- You'll also want to discern if the therapist has worked with religious couples, and if they can be respectful to your Christian orientation. To that end, if the subject doesn't come up, you should ask if the therapist believes he/she can be respectful to your religious tradition and value system. If circumstances warrant, you might want to also ask if the therapist would be willing to collaborate with your pastor. A pastor's perspective can often prove insightful and useful during this process.

- When you finally make a decision and begin couples' therapy, it's important that you commit yourself to the work. If you or your partner remains halfheartedly committed to the work—and we do mean "work"—or become easily discouraged, then even the most skilled therapist will not be able to help you.

- You'll also want to find someone who doesn't sit back too much during the sessions. From our perspective, couples' work requires the therapist to be very active. The therapist must probe and constantly challenge respectfully. If this doesn't happen early into the therapy process, you may want to consider a change.

- Last, but not least, even when couples are committed to the therapeutic process and the therapist is well-equipped to do the work, it will take some time for therapy to work—somewhere between ten and fifteen sessions is a good estimate. However, while the full effects of therapy may take time, if after five-seven sessions, you don't begin to make some progress, ask the therapist to explain their treatment plan. If you are not satisfied with what you hear, before investing too much more time and money, you should consider the pros and cons of searching for another therapist.

Appendix II

A Brief Summary of the Sacrament of Marriage

Before discussing the Sacrament of Marriage, we would like to provide you with a working definition of a sacrament from an Orthodox perspective. If you desire more information, here are some other helpful resources.

Ware, T. *The Orthodox Church.* London: Penguin Books, 1997.

Coniaris, A. *These Are the Sacraments.* Minneapolis, MN: Light and Life Publishing Company, 1981.

Meyendorff, J. *Byzantine Theology: Historical Trends and Doctrinal Themes.* New York: Fordham University Press, 1979.

Chamberas, P. *This Is a Great Mystery: Christian Marriage in the Orthodox Church.* Brookline, MA: Metropolis of Boston, 2003.

The sacraments can be understood as God-given points of contact, where God makes Himself present and available to us on a personal level. As we choose to faithfully participate in these mysteries, God's life-giving, life-changing grace touches our lives and, by extension, makes us holy. The sacraments have either been instituted by Christ or the apostles. Orthodox Tradition also refers to them as mysteries because in and through the sacramental life of the Church we have a direct encounter with God.

Some History

The Sacrament of Marriage is comprised of two interrelated parts—the Betrothal Service and the Crowning Service. It evolved over a number of centuries. Up until the ninth century, marriages were blessed during the Divine Liturgy. Thereafter, marriages were blessed outside of the Eucharist. By the end of the sixteenth century, the sacrament, as we know it, was being celebrated. Prior to this, shorter variations of the sacrament were conducted.

The Sacrament of Marriage

Despite these historical variations, the Church has always understood marriage as intimately related to our personal spiritual journey. Above and beyond the legal, psychological and sociological dimensions that society typically identifies as part and parcel of marriage, the Church expands the definition of marriage and describes it as a holy union whereby a man and woman struggle together toward sanctification and eternal life within a community of faithful called the Church. As we will see, the symbolism, prayers, and rituals that unfold during the Betrothal Service, as well as the Sacrament of Marriage, serve to reinforce, communicate, and celebrate this central meaning of marriage.

Your journey of marriage begins as the two of you stand at the front of the church. Your presence in the front of the community is a pledge that you are making to each other that marriage is a journey together. You are making this pledge in the presence of family and friends. Even the smallest weddings require a best man and maid of honor, or sponsors. This is not done for legalistic reasons, but to communicate a deep truth about the journey of marriage.

Marriage is not a private affair. It is a community event and, as a sacrament, it is intimately connected to the Church community. Your marriage will affect a lot of people, and when marriages fail, the whole community is affected. While marriage is personal and intimate, it is not private. We are not meant to be alone at the ceremony, and we are not meant to be alone on the journey of marriage. The members of the community communicate their love and support by their presence and prayers at the wedding service, and that love and support is necessary on the journey of marriage.

As you stand before the altar, in front of you will be a small table. On that table you will see the Gospel book, and on the Gospel book will be your wedding rings and your wedding crowns. This placement is intentional and symbolic. It is a silent witness to the fact that your marriage is supported and sustained by Christ, the Word of God. It is upon Christ that our marriages must be built. It is Christ who needs to be the foundation of a Christian marriage.

The Betrothal Service

The first part of the service is referred to as the Betrothal Service. It is comprised of a series of petitions, a few short prayers, the exchange of the rings and a lengthy prayer. Here are the main components:

- Doxology

- Opening Petitions

- Two Short Prayers

- The Exchange of Rings

- The Closing Prayer

Let's briefly examine the components of this service, while keeping in mind that these various pieces are interrelated and should not be understood apart from one another. Together, they lead the couple to an experience that is greater than the sum of its parts.

Doxology

"Blessed be our God both now and ever and unto the ages of ages." Many Orthodox prayer services begin with this doxology. This is a form of prayer. As you may have already noticed, this prayer does not request anything from God. It simply calls both partners—together with all who are in attendance—to acknowledge and glorify God. It is a natural response that faithful people have when they stand before God.

Opening Petitions

A petition is a form of prayer. Since many of our prayers tend to be offered to God in the form of requests or petitions, this type of prayer is perhaps the most familiar to most people, "Dear God, please help me today," is a simple example of this type of prayer.

These petitions begin with some general requests asking God to bless those in attendance with peace and salvation. The priest then asks God to be mindful of our world, the Church, and our leaders. After these opening petitions, the list quickly narrows its focus and concerns itself with the man and woman pledging themselves to one another.

"For the servants of God _____ and _____, who now pledge themselves to one another, and for their salvation, let us pray to the Lord."

The first prayer specifically for the couple is for their salvation. As we discuss in the seminar, marriage is a journey of salvation.

The very next petition reads, *"That there may be sent upon them peaceful and perfect love, and protection, let us pray to the Lord."*

Marriage is a journey of acquiring perfect love for each other, which is a gift from God as we journey together with Him.

The remaining prayers will ask God to bless the couple with divine peace, faith, harmony, purity, and oneness of mind. These prayers also petition God to bless the couple with children, while promoting fidelity and mutual trust within their lives across the life cycle. These are all indispensable personal and couple needs, which are based on Christian values and virtues that promote oneness and marital happiness.

Two Short Prayers

The priest will subsequently read two short prayers. These prayers reflect the Church's understanding that God's love has brought them together and will sustain them in *"peace and oneness of mind"* across the marital life cycle. The priest compares the relationship between the bride and groom to the relationship between God and the Church. This image of God as the faithful Bridegroom and humanity as His bride communicates the Church's understanding of the significance of marriage: it is modeled on God's relationship with humanity.

The Exchange of Rings

The priest will stand before the couple and bless them in the sign of the cross with their wedding rings. Beginning with the groom, he will prayerfully intone the following statement: *"The servant of God _____ is betrothed to the servant of God _____ in the name of the Father, Son, and Holy Spirit."* This will be done three times. Once this step is complete, the priest will begin with the bride, prayerfully repeating the same pattern. After the priest places the rings on the bride and groom, the sponsor will exchange the rings.

This liturgical action serves to seal the couple's commitment. No vows are requested or required. The couple's silent participation in this rite presupposes their commitment and, from an Orthodox perspective, is a more than sufficient witness of their dedication to one another. The rings they will wear on their fingers henceforth will serve as a silent reminder of this commitment.

The mutual exchange of rings is an expression of the mutual self-offering between a husband and wife, essential for oneness in marriage. No longer are the bride and groom independent individuals but rather two interdependent persons who belong to each other and rely on each other to grow in wholeness. Marriage is a journey of becoming one.

The Closing Prayer

The final prayer serves to provide closure by recapping some of the significant underlying meaning of the rings. The rings symbolize the authority, glory, and honor that the couple are bound, mutually, to preserve and uphold. Numerous Old Testament references remind the couple that it is God who will bless and support their commitment and guide their future footsteps as He protected and guided other faithful individuals and couples before them. We ask God to *"confirm the word of promise,"* and *"make them secure in that holy unity which is accomplished by You."* It is God who not only blesses the union but unites the couple as one.

The rings reflect God's merciful love, which he showers upon the couple, promising to stand by the couple and provide them with his care. The prayer references the *"right hand of God,"* and the "*word of God,*" which symbolize His power. The same God who created the universe is involved now directly in the life of the bride and groom. Successful marriage depends upon God's promise to unite and sustain the marital union. Where human promises are limited, God's promise is never-failing.

This prayer also functions to provide a convenient transition into the second half of the service. One of the final phrases alludes to the couple's life together as husband and wife, a life that will continue to be blessed by God: *"and may Your angel go before them all the days of their life, for you are He that blesses and sanctifies all things."*

The Crowning Service

This service is comprised of the following parts: (1) Psalm 127/128, (2) Doxology, (3) Petitions, (4) Prayers, (5) Crowning, (6) Scripture Readings, (7) Lord's Prayer, (8) Common Cup, (9) Procession, and (10) Final Exhortation and Dismissal. While it is important to understand each of these components, a fuller understanding of the service emerges when these various parts are integrated and experienced as a whole.

Psalm 127/128

The Service of the Crowning begins with the singing of Psalm 127, which celebrates the blessings that come from family life lived according to God's commandments. From an early age, our society teaches us that we are responsible for our own happiness and prosperity, and increasingly couples put off having children because of the perception that children are a burden and undermine marital happiness. This psalm disagrees with these assertions and reminds couples that true happiness and prosperity come from seeking to live godly lives and that children are blessings from God.

Doxology

"Blessed is the Kingdom of the Father, Son, and Holy Spirit, now and ever and unto the ages of ages."

This proclamation is the same proclamation that begins each Divine Liturgy and Baptism in the Orthodox Church. Originally, baptisms and weddings were performed within the context of the Sunday Liturgy. While this is no longer the practice, these two sacraments have maintained this opening proclamation, as well as an orientation toward the Kingdom of Heaven. Marriage is a journey to heaven. Through marriage, God transforms our human love into the divine love of the Kingdom of God. It is this transformation in divine love that enables a husband and wife to grow, daily, in love for each other and for God, unto the ages of ages.

The Wedding Candles

After the doxology the priest will present the wedding candles to both partners and instruct them to hold them in their right hands—the right hand reminds us of Christ who ascended into heaven and sits at the right hand of God the Father. The candle flame symbolizes divine light that has come into the world through Christ. Through this ritual the couple celebrates the light of Christ that has come into the world to illumine their lives as individuals, as well as the mutual joining together of their lives as a couple in Christ.

Petitions

After the introductory petitions, a series of requests are made on behalf of both the bride and the groom. The first of these petitions will include both individuals' names to emphasize the personal characteristic of the sacrament. This petition begins, *"For the servants of God _____ and _____...."* It reminds us that God knows us and loves us personally and is personally involved in our journey of marriage.

The other petitions are intended to help the couple understand that they are being united to one another in a community of marriage that will, at once, be separate and a part of a larger community of faithful individuals, couples, and families. These prayers also ask Christ to be present in the couple's marriage, as He was present and blessed the marriage He attended in Cana (John 2:1-11). They further emphasize the importance of children and ask God to bless each couple with *"fruit of the womb"* in accordance with His wisdom.

Three Prayers

Along with the other prayers in this service, the next three lengthy prayers tell a wonderful story. With the help of a series of Old Testament images, metaphors and references, the story they describe involves a loving, caring God who preserved and protected these couples to fulfill His plan for the coming of Christ and the salvation of the world. These prayers also recount how marriage affords us the opportunity to become a part of this larger story in a very personal way, bringing our marriage under the care and protection of God for our salvation. From this God-given institution, a new relationship is formed, and from this willful joining together, two lives are prayerfully bonded together and children emerge, destined to become, for themselves, children of God.

The commandment to *"be fruitful and multiply,"* mentioned in the first prayer, is a reference to God's blessing and command to Adam and Eve in Genesis, yet it takes on special meaning within the sacrament of marriage. To be fruitful (in Greek αυξάνεσθε) means, more precisely, to grow and to become perfect, and to multiply (πληθύνεσθε) means to make full, or increase, not just in quantity but in quality. In this sense, the blessing to be fruitful and multiply, beyond simply referring to having children, refers to marriage as a journey of husband and wife growing together in mutual fullness and perfection as they are transformed in divine love for each other.

Additionally, as the last of these three prayers is read and the telling of the story begins to draw to a close, the priest will stand before the couple and read, "*O Sovereign Lord, stretch forth Your hand from your Holy dwelling place, and join together this Your servant _____ and Your servant _____.*" He will then join their right hands together, and through this invocation and ritual another couple is brought into this story coupled with the Church's hope and prayer that they will make this story an integral part of the story they will coauthor together into the future.

"Unite them, O Lord, to have oneness of mind," the priest will pray, and the congregation will concur with an *"Amen,"* reflecting the nature of marriage as a journey of becoming one.

The Crowning

After the couple's right hands are joined together, the priest will bless their wedding crowns over the Gospel book, then bless the groom with the crowns and recite the following statement three times in front of the couple: *"The servant of God _____ is crowned to the servant of God _____, in the name of the Father and the Son and the Holy Spirit."* Upon completion, he will repeat the process, beginning with the bride while repeating the same words. The priest will then place the wedding crowns on both partners' heads while chanting a verse from Psalm 8, *"O, Lord our God, crown them with glory and honor."* The sponsor will then exchange the crowns three times and place them back on each partner's head. Although this is an ancient ritual, the use of crowns is a biblical tradition.

The crowns are a sign of victory. Athletes in ancient times received a victory wreath after competing in the same way that Olympians today receive a gold medal. St. Paul uses the image of crowns to encourage Christians to struggle to receive *"an imperishable wreath as athletes for Christ"* (I Corinthians 9:24–25). In this way, the crowns are an expression of the divine reward for faithfulness to Christ in this life. Crowns are associated with those who give up their life for Christ. In the account of the forty martyrs mentioned in the second prayer before the crowning, crowns descended upon each of them just before they offered their lives up to Christ.

The use of crowns in marriage reflects the Church's understanding that marriage is a type of martyrdom, a type of self-sacrifice that is no less a martyrdom than that of the Christians who died for Christ. This is not to say that marriage is a journey of suffering. Note how many references there are, throughout the wedding ceremony, to the couple living in peace, harmony, and happiness. The martyrdom of marriage is a martyrdom of giving up our own way and our own desires and, out of love, seeking to serve each other.

"O Lord our God, crown them with glory and honor," chants the priest, invoking God to send His Holy Spirit upon the couple. In ancient times, monarchs' crowns symbolized their absolute rule over their kingdom. Similarly, in this liturgical ritual Christ installs the couple over their household as king and queen, with one important difference. Unlike the manipulative, controlling style of rule that many kings and queens personified, this service calls both spouses to rule over their household in a Christlike manner employing Christian virtues like humility, kindness, patience, and self-sacrificial love. Real glory and honor come through this type of self-giving and sacrificial love within married life.

Scripture Readings

"Be subject to one another out of reverence for Christ," we hear from the Epistle reading of the service, reinforcing this central theme of marriage. The readings are carefully selected because they are foundational to the Orthodox Church's understanding of marriage. They encapsulate much of what the Orthodox Church believes about marriage and reinforce the message behind the prayers and hymns of this service. There are two Scripture readings from the New Testament in this service.

The first reading comes from the Letter to the Ephesians (5:20–33). This reading focuses on the new life of the husband and wife in Christ, modeled after Christ's relationship with the Church. Husbands and wives are called to subject themselves to each other and love each other, modeled after Christ and His love for humanity. The different roles of husband and wife find their meaning in the context of a fundamental equality and mutuality of the persons of the husband and wife. This context is central to an Orthodox perspective of marriage and is essential for a healthy marriage.

The second reading from Saint John's Gospel (2:1–11) is the account of Jesus at the wedding of Cana. Christ's presence at this wedding is an affirmation and a blessing, by God, of marriage. Christ not only attended the wedding, but when the host of the wedding ran out of wine, Christ performed the first miracle of his ministry by turning water into wine. In addition to the practical meaning of this miracle, the Church understands this miracle as reflecting something deeper about Christ's presence in all our marriages. Human love will dry up as we journey in marriage, yet when we bring to him the water of our struggles and mistakes in marriage, He turns it into the wine of divine love. He fills our hearts to overflowing, and the more we journey in His love, the more our hearts are filled with the best wine of divine love.

Petitions and the Lord's Prayer

Now that the couple has been crowned, attention is turned to praying for this new union. Specifically, the priest will pray for peace, concord, purity, and chastity in their relationship. By praying for chastity, specifically, the Church recognizes the special role of physical intimacy in marriage. Chastity in this sense is not the absence of physical relations. The Church blesses this dimension of marriage and prays that the couple's physical relations will be an expression of the same mutual self-giving and love that are at the heart of marriage and have been expressed throughout the wedding service.

After these petitions and prayers are recited, the congregation prays the Lord's Prayer. Jesus Christ offered this prayer to the disciples when they asked, "Teach us to pray" (Luke 11:1). This is a familiar prayer that Christians repeat at many different times and places, and couples are encouraged to pray this prayer together daily. At any given place and time, the words in this prayer serve to comfort them and remind them of God's presence in their lives.

The Common Cup

The priest will then ask God to bless a cup that contains wine. This cup is called the Common Cup. He will then offer the cup to each partner. Each partner will drink from the cup three times as the communion hymn, *"I shall drink of the cup of salvation, and call upon the name of the Lord,"* is chanted. Briefly, the wine in this cup symbolizes the bitter and sweet moments of married life that both partners will share together on their marriage journey. This ritual also reminds the couple that God will bless them throughout the marital and family life cycle in their journey of salvation.

Procession

After the couple drink from the Common Cup, the priest, couple, and sponsor will process around the table. In earlier times, this procession took place from the church to the couple's home. Today, it takes place around a table in the center of the solea, in front of the icon screen.

Holding the book of Gospels in his right hand, the priest will guide the procession around the table three times while three hymns are chanted. As the couple follow the priest, their journey of marriage begins, but it is not a journey they will take alone. The Gospel book that the priest holds and the presence of their guests serve to remind them that their marriage journey is to be guided by Christ Himself and will include the priest as well as those who love and support them. Further, the joyous hymns chanted as they process around the table remind the couple of their communion with Christ and the saints and the sacrificial nature of marriage.

Final Exhortation

Two short congratulatory prayers are read immediately following the procession. Unlike all the other prayers of the service, which are directed to God, these prayers are directed, specifically, to the bride and the groom. These exhortations are the liturgical congratulations and greetings of the new couple by the priest. The first relates to the groom and the second to the bride. In each case, both partners are asked to emulate the faith of several Old Testament figures who found happiness and marital fulfillment through their faith in God. The crowns are then removed from their heads and placed on the altar.

Finally, in the dismissal that follows we pray that God and all the saints accompany the new couple on their journey to heaven and provide for them all good things of earthly life. We see here, and throughout the service, that when we keep our focus on Christ, He provides for all our earthly needs as we grow, over a lifetime together, closer to Him and closer to each other.

Appendix III

Recommended Readings

Orthodox Resources

Chamberas, P. *This Is a Great Mystery: Christian Marriage in the Orthodox Church.* Brookline, MA: Metropolis of Boston, 2003.

Chrysostom, J. *On Marriage and Family Life.* Catherine P. Roth and David Anderson, (trns.) New York: SVS Press, 2003.

Evdokimov, P. *The Sacrament of Love.* New York: SVS Press, 1995.

Joanides, C. *When You Intermarry: A Resource for Inter-Christian, Intercultural Couples, Parents and Families.* New York: Greek Orthodox Archdiocese of America, 2002.

Joanides, C. *Attending to Your Marriage: A Resource for Christian Couples.* Minneapolis, MN: Light and Life Publishing Company, 2006.

Mack, J. *Preserve Them, O Lord.* Ben Lomond, CA: Conciliar Press, 2005.

Meyendorff, J. *Marriage: An Orthodox Perspective.* New York: SVS Press, 2000.

Additional Resources

Chapman, G. *The Five Love Languages: How to Express Heartfelt Commitment to Your Mate.* Chicago: Northfield Publishing, 2004.

Glass, S. P. *Not Just Friends: Rebuilding Trust and Recovering Your Sanity After Infidelity.* New York: Free Press, 2003.

Gottman, J. M., and N. Silver. *The Seven Principles for Making Marriage Work.* New York: Three Rivers Press, 1991.

Gottman, J. M., and J. DeClaire. *The Relationship Cure: A 5 Step Guide for Building Better Connections with Family, Friends, and Lovers.* New York: Crown Publishers, 2001.

Kendrick, S., A. Kendrick, and L. Kimbrough. *The Love Dare.* Nashville, TN: B & H Publishing, 2008.

Love, P., and S. Stosney. *How to Improve Your Marriage Without Talking About It.* New York: Broadway Books, 2007.

Markman, H., and S. Stanley. *Fighting for Your Marriage: Deluxe and Revised Edition.* San Francisco, CA: Jossey-Bass Publishers, 2010.

Markman, H., S. Stanley, S. Blumberg, and N. Jenkins. *12 Hours to a Great Marriage.* San Francisco, CA: Jossey-Bass Publishers, 2004.

McCarthy, B., and E. McCarthy. *Rekindling Desire: A Step-by-Step Program to Help Low-Sex and No-Sex Marriages.* New York: Brunner-Routledge, 2003.

Stanley, S., D. Tratheon, S. McCain, and M. Bryan. *A Lasting Promise: A Christian Guide to Fighting for Your Marriage.* San Francisco, CA: Jossey-Bass Publishers, 1998.

Thomas, G. *Sacred Marriage.* Grand Rapids, MI: Zondervan, 2000.

Weiner-Davis, M. *Divorce Remedy.* New York: Simon & Schuster, 2001.

About the Authors

Philip Mamalakis, Ph.D., LMFT, lives with his wife, Georgia, and seven children, in Boston, Massachusetts, where he is the Assistant Professor of Pastoral Care at Holy Cross Greek Orthodox School of Theology. Dr. Mamalakis directs the Field Education Program and teaches classes on pastoral care, counseling, grief, death, and dying.

Dr. Mamalakis offers seminars, retreats, and lectures on marriage, family life, and parenting in the Orthodox Church. He sits on the Family Ministry Committee of the Boston Metropolis and has been conducting marriage preparation seminars in the Boston area. He is currently offering training for those interested in facilitating marriage preparation seminars in the Archdiocese based on this book, *The Journey of Marriage in the Orthodox Church.*

Dr. Mamalakis has an M.Div. from Holy Cross and a Ph.D. from Purdue University in child development and family studies, specializing in marriage and family therapy. He has written numerous articles and book chapters on Orthodox marriage, family life, and contemporary mental health.

He is a licensed marriage and family therapist and a clinical member of the American Association of Marriage and Family Therapy (AAMFT) with a private counseling practice in Newton, Massachusetts, where he works with individuals, couples and families.

Rev. Fr. Charles Joanides, Ph.D., LMFT, was ordained to the priesthood in 1980. He has served several parishes across the Greek Orthodox Archdiocese (GOA) since then. He is married and both he and Presvytera Nancy have two children, Stephan (30) and Sara (28) and are the grandparents of one.

Father Charles is currently directing the GOA's ministry to intermarried couples and their families. Much of his work can be accessed on the Interfaith Marriage Web site at www.interfaith.goarch.org. In addition, Fr. Charles teaches marriage and family therapy at Nyack College in New York.

He holds a B.A. from the University of Massachusetts, an M-Div from Hellenic College/Holy Cross, an M.A. in Human Development and Family Relations with a specialty in Marriage and Family Therapy from the University of Connecticut, and a Ph.D. in Human Development and Family Studies with a specialty in Marriage and Family Therapy from Iowa State University.

Father Charles has authored the following books: *When You Intermarry: A Resource for Inter-Christian, Intercultural Couples, Parents and Families, Ministering to Intermarried Couples: A Resource for Clergy and Lay Workers,* and *Attending to Your Marriage: A Resource for Christian Couples.* His writings have also appeared in numerous professional journals, magazines and newspapers.

Father Charles is a licensed marriage and family therapist, a clinical member of the American Association of Marriage and Family Therapists (AAMFT) and an approved AAMFT supervisor. He has a small private practice specializing in reclaiming marriages.